Alas, poor Yorick! I knew him, Horatio. A fellow of infinite jest, of most excellent fancy. He hath borne me on his back a thousand times. And now, how abhorred in my imagination it is! My gorge rises at it. Here hung those lips that I have kissed I know not how oft. Where be your gibes now? your gambols? your songs? your flashes of merriment that were wont to set the table on a roar? Not one now, to mock your own grinning?

HAMLET
Act V, Scene 1

The Tragedy of Hamlet

with Connections

The Tragedy
of Hamlet

William Shakespeare

with
Connections

HOLT, RINEHART AND WINSTON
Harcourt Brace & Company

Austin · New York · Orlando · Atlanta · San Francisco
Boston · Dallas · Toronto · London

For permission to reprint copyrighted material, grateful acknowledgment is made to the following sources:

Doubleday, a division of Random House, Inc.: "In a Dark Time" from *The Collected Poems of Theodore Roethke.* Copyright © 1960 by Beatrice Roethke, Administratrix of the Estate of Theodore Roethke. **HarperCollins Publishers:** From "Plays and Performances" from *Shakespeare and His Theatre* by John Russell Brown. Copyright © 1982 by John Russell Brown. **The New York Times Company:** Review of *Hamlet* by Bosley Crowther from *The New York Times* September 30, 1948 from *The New York Times Film Reviews.* Copyright © 1948 by The New York Times Company. **Gerald W. Purcell Associated, Ltd.:** "Mourning Grace" from *The Complete Collected Poems of Maya Angelou.* Copyright © 1969 by Maya Angelou. **Random House, Inc.:** "Insomniac" from *Shaker, Why Don't You Sing* by Maya Angelou. Copyright © 1983 by Maya Angelou. **Richard L. Sterne:** From "The First Week of Rehearsals" from *John Gielgud Directs Richard Burton in Hamlet: A Journal of Rehearsals* by Richard L. Sterne. Copyright © 1967 by Richard L. Sterne. **Universal Press Syndicate:** From two reviews of *Hamlet* by Roger Ebert from ROGER EBERT'S column (retitled "The Branagh *Hamlet*" and "The Gibson *Hamlet*") from *Chicago Sun Times Reviews,* January 1991 and January 1997. Copyright © 1991, 1997 by Universal Press Syndicate. All rights reserved. **Jonathan Vos Post:** From "Raymond Chandler's Hamlet" by Jonathan Vos Post from Emerald City website, September 2, 1999. Copyright © 1999 by Jonathan Vos Post. Available at http://www.magicdragon.com/ EmeraldCity/Mystery/Chandler-Hamlet.html. **Donald A. Yates:** "Just Lather, That's All" by Hernando Téllez, translated by Donald A. Yates.

Cover art: Joe Melomo, Design Director; Shoehorn, Inc., Designer; Andrew Yates, Photographer; Betty Mayo, Photo Researcher

HRW is a registered trademark licensed to Holt, Rinehart and Winston.

Printed in the United States of America

ISBN 0-03-095769-9

16 17 018 10 09 08 07

Contents

CONTINUED

On the Origins of *Hamlet*
from *Shakespeare of London*
Marchette Chute

The unauthorized first edition of *Hamlet,* which was
ready for publication in July, 1602, and published in a
very bad text the following year, announced on its title
page that it had been many times acted "in the City of
London, as also in the two Universities of Cambridge and
Oxford." It must have been in the towns of Oxford and
Cambridge, rather than in the university section, that
Hamlet was acted, and the students who went to the inn-
yards to see it must have gone very quietly.

Since the hero of Shakespeare's play was himself a
university product, his views on the drama were those
of any well-educated young intellectual of the period.
Hamlet had nothing but scorn for the groundlings, and
his idea of true theater was to hear the sorrows of the
characters described at secondhand in dignified and inter-
minable blank verse. Nothing could be more distasteful
to any well-educated Renaissance gentleman, from Sir
Philip Sidney down, than to have an actor play Hecuba
by running about the stage in indecorous agony, with a
blanket about the queen's hips and Troy burning behind
her. The proper thing to do was to describe her from afar,
and the play from which Hamlet quotes so admiringly
represents the best practices of university stagecraft, with
Hecuba's agony filtered to the audience at secondhand
through Senecan blank verse. It was the penny public, the
groundlings, who demanded a full view onstage of Hecuba's
agony and who encouraged the sprawling, violent dramas
of which the universities so thoroughly disapproved. It is
a sobering thought that Hamlet the playgoer would not

have approved of *Hamlet* the play, with its mixture of comedy and tragedy, its failure to observe the unities, and all its other sins against decorum that any young gentleman from the universities would have noticed immediately.

The plot into which Shakespeare inserted his intellectual young student from the university of Wittenberg was a shabby old melodrama that had been in the repertoire of the Chamberlain's company for a long time and had evidently been written about the time when Shakespeare first came up to London. The ghost who went around wailing, "Hamlet, revenge," was a byword in the late 80's, and a play that Shakespeare's company produced the year the Globe was built managed to be very amusing at the expense of this kind of antiquated drama.

> A filthy ghost
> Lapt in some foul sheet, or a leather pilch,
> Comes screaming in like a pig half sticked
> And cries, *Vindicta*—Revenge, Revenge!

Shakespeare, as usual, knew what he was doing. It was not the first time he had used shoddy material as the springboard for a play, and in this case his actor's eye saw the special uses of the situation. The bloody, barbaric old plot gave him a dark backdrop for the unhappy young modernist who was his hero, and his hero's temperament in turn gave him a solution for the chief difficulty confronting any dramatist who worked in the field of revenge tragedy. Unless there was some reason why the revenge was delayed, the play would be over in the first act; and a revenge hero like Hamlet, caught in the general backwash of gloom and indecision that characterized the final years of Elizabeth's reign, was exactly the sort of man who was incapable of working himself up to a single course of action until he had succeeded in ruining the lives of everyone in the cast.

Hamlet was born in part of the young men who had been glooming about the universities and the Inns of Court in the *fin di siècle* atmosphere of the late 90's and passing remarks on the hollowness of life, the futility of heroic action and the degrading nature of sexual intercourse; but he was also the product of a more specialized group that was interesting the doctors of the period. A competent London Physician like Timothy Bright would have diagnosed Hamlet as a melancholic and put much of his "internal darkness" down to physical causes. Melancholics, as Dr. Bright explained, "be not so apt for action." They are "given to fearful and terrible dreams," are "exact and curious in pondering," are "sometimes furious and sometimes merry," and are "out of measure passionate." They have frequently studied too much, they mistrust their memories, and they dislike color in their clothes.

This sort of information was useful to Shakespeare as a kind of springboard, but it was no more than that. He was not like George Chapman, who was very learned in Elizabethan theories of psychology and loaded his heroes with them. Shakespeare did not work from theories but from people. He knew that Hamlet's dilemma, between the flesh and the spirit, was at the heart of every human being's private tragedy, and he made Hamlet so terrifyingly real, with his courtesy and his violence, his intelligence and his self-hatred, his inconsistencies and his terrors, that every generation since has been able to recognize in him its own image.

The actors of the Chamberlain's company must have realized, sometime during rehearsals, that they had been given the script of one of those astonishing plays that please everyone. If they did not, the reaction of the audience would have told them soon enough. Even at its lowest level, *Hamlet* is a magnificently constructed piece of melodrama, with enough blood and pageantry and swordplay to please the sleepiest ten-year-old; and at its highest it travels so far into the secret countries of the heart that even the wisest should be able to see a new landscape unfolding in front of him.

Echoes of the play's success in the contemporary theaters still exist. Anthony Scoloker introduced a book of his by remarking that any piece of writing should ideally be like Sidney's *Arcadia,* which was still the most admired work of the period. "Or, to come home to the vulgar's element, like friendly Shakespeare's tragedies. . . . Faith, it should please all, like Prince Hamlet." Gabriel Harvey, who had once argued literary theory with his friend Sidney and was still respected as a scholar, used a blank space in his copy of Chaucer to jot down in his neat handwriting a few comments on the current literary scene. He noted that "the younger sort take much delight in Shakespeare's *Venus and Adonis;* but his *Lucrece,* and his *Hamlet, Prince of Denmark* have it in them to please the wiser sort." *Lucrece* was in its fourth edition and was generally conceded to be the best thing its author had ever written; to link it with a common play from the boards of the Globe theater was an almost unheard-of concession for a literary man to make.

Shakespeare poured a kind of lavishness into *Hamlet* that is in direct contrast to the spareness of his *Julius Caesar. Hamlet* is the longest play he ever wrote and has by far the largest vocabulary of new words, and the cutting of the play for normal stage production must have posed a difficult problem.

Dramatis Personae

KING CLAUDIUS, King of Denmark.

HAMLET, son to the late, and nephew to the present king.

LORD POLONIUS, Lord Chamberlain.

HORATIO, friend to Hamlet.

LAERTES, son to Polonius.

LUCIANUS, nephew to the king.

VOLTEMAND, CORNELIUS, ROSENCRANTZ, GUILDENSTERN,
OSRIC, A GENTLEMAN, courtiers.

PRIEST.

MARCELLUS, BERNARDO, officers.

FRANCISCO, a soldier.

REYNALDO, servant to Polonius.

FIRST PLAYER, PLAYER KING, PLAYER QUEEN, players.

FIRST CLOWN, SECOND CLOWN, grave diggers.

PRINCE FORTINBRAS, Prince of Norway.

A Norwegian Captain.

English Ambassadors.

QUEEN GERTRUDE, Queen of Denmark, and mother to
Hamlet.

OPHELIA, daughter to Polonius.

Lords, Ladies, Officers, Soldiers, Sailors, Messengers,
and other Attendants.

GHOST of Hamlet's Father.

Act I

Scene 1. *Elsinore. A platform before the castle.*

FRANCISCO *at his post. Enter* BERNARDO.

Bernardo. Who's there?
Francisco.
    Nay, answer me. Stand and unfold° yourself.
Bernardo. Long live the King!
Francisco. Bernardo?
Bernardo. He.   5
Francisco.
    You come most carefully upon your hour.°
Bernardo.
    'Tis now struck twelve. Get thee to bed, Francisco.
Francisco.
    For this relief much thanks. 'Tis bitter cold,
    And I am sick at heart.
Bernardo.
    Have you had quiet guard?
Francisco.   Not a mouse stirring.   10
Bernardo.
    Well, good night.
    If you do meet Horatio and Marcellus,
    The rivals° of my watch, bid them make haste.

Enter HORATIO *and* MARCELLUS.

I.1.2. **unfold:** reveal.
6.   **You … hour:** You have arrived very promptly.
13.   **rivals:** partners.

Francisco.
    I think I hear them. Stand, ho! Who is there?
Horatio.
    Friends to this ground.
Marcellus.   And liegemen to the Dane.°   15
Francisco.
    Give you good night.
Marcellus.   O, farewell, honest soldier.
    Who hath relieved you?
Francisco.   Bernardo has my place.
    Give you good night.

                                         Exit.

Marcellus.   Holla, Bernardo!
Bernardo.   Say—
    What, is Horatio there?
Horatio.   A piece of him.°
Bernardo.
    Welcome, Horatio. Welcome, good Marcellus.   20
Marcellus.
        What, has this thing appeared again tonight?
Bernardo.
    I have seen nothing.
Marcellus.
    Horatio says 'tis but our fantasy,
    And will not let belief take hold of him
    Touching this dreaded sight, twice seen of us.   25
    Therefore I have entreated him along,
    With us to watch the minutes of this night,
    That, if again this apparition come,
    He may approve° our eyes and speak to it.°

---

15.   **liegemen … Dane:** loyal subjects of the king.
19.   **A piece of him:** Horatio, who doubts the existence of a ghost, is there
        in body but not in spirit.
29.   **approve:** verify. **speak to it:** The belief was that a ghost could not
        speak until spoken to. Marcellus assumes the ghost wants to talk but
        has not yet done so because no one has addressed it.

Horatio.

Tush, tush, 'twill not appear.

Bernardo. Sit down awhile,   30

And let us once again assail your ears,

That are so fortified against our story,

What we two nights have seen.

Horatio. Well, sit we down,

And let us hear Bernardo speak of this.

Bernardo.

Last night of all,   35

When yond same star that's westward from the pole°

Had made his° course t' illume° that part of heaven

Where now it burns, Marcellus and myself,

The bell then beating one—

Enter GHOST.

Marcellus.

Peace! break thee off! Look where it comes again!   40

Bernardo.

In the same figure, like° the King that's dead.

Marcellus.

Thou art a scholar;° speak to it, Horatio.

Bernardo.

Looks it not like the King? Mark it, Horatio.

Horatio.

Most like. It harrows° me with fear and wonder.

Bernardo.

It would be spoke to.

Marcellus. Question it, Horatio.   45

---

36.   **pole:** Polaris, the North Star.
37.   **his:** an older form of the pronoun *its. His* was the possessive of both *he* and *it.* **t' illume:** to light.
41.   **like:** resembling.
42.   **scholar:** learned person who would know how to question a ghost.
44:   **harrows:** distresses, lacerates.

Horatio.

What art thou that usurp'st° this time of night
Together with° that fair and warlike form
In which the majesty of buried Denmark°
Did sometimes march? By heaven I charge thee speak!

Marcellus.

It is offended.

Bernardo.　　　See, it stalks away!　　　　　　　50

Horatio.

Stay! Speak, speak! I charge thee, speak!

Exit GHOST.

Marcellus.

'Tis gone, and will not answer.°

Bernardo.

How now, Horatio? You tremble and look pale.
Is not this something more than fantasy?
What think you on't?　　　　　　　　　　55

Horatio.

Before my God, I might not this believe
Without the sensible and true avouch°
Of mine own eyes.

Marcellus.　　　　　Is it not like the King?

Horatio.

As thou art to thyself.
Such was the very armor he had on　　　　60
When he the ambitious Norway combated;
So frowned he once when, in an angry parle,°
He smote the sledded Polacks° on the ice.
'Tis strange.

46.　**usurp'st:** takes over.
47.　**Together with:** appearing in.
48.　**the majesty … Denmark:** the now-dead King of Denmark.
52.　**'Tis … answer:** A ghost speaks only to one it has a message for.
　　　It is "offended" (line 50) because it has no business with Horatio.
57.　**sensible:** sensory. **avouch:** evidence.
62.　**parle:** parley, conference.
63.　**sledded Polacks:** Poles using sleds.

Marcellus.
>Thus twice before, and jump° at this dead hour,   65
>With martial stalk hath he gone by our watch.

Horatio.
>In what particular thought to work I know not;
>But in the gross and scope of my opinion,°
>This bodes some strange eruption to our state.

Marcellus.
>Good now,° sit down, and tell me he that knows,   70
>Why this same strict and most observant watch
>So nightly toils the subject of the land,
>And why such daily cast of brazen cannon
>And foreign mart for implements of war;
>Why such impress of shipwrights, whose sore task   75
>Does not divide the Sunday from the week;°
>What might be toward,° that this sweaty haste
>Doth make the night joint-laborer with the day?°
>Who is't that can inform me?

Horatio.   That can I.
>At least, the whisper goes so. Our last King,   80
>Whose image even but now appeared to us,
>Was, as you know, by Fortinbras of Norway,
>Thereto pricked on by a most emulate pride,°
>Dared to the combat; in which our valiant Hamlet
>(For so this side of our known world esteemed him)   85
>Did slay this Fortinbras; who, by a sealed compact,
>Well ratified by law and heraldry,°
>Did forfeit, with his life, all those his lands

---

65.   **jump:** precisely.
67–68. **In ... opinion:** I don't know what to think, but I'm of the
       opinion that.
70.   **Good now:** Please.
75–76. **whose ... week:** who are working seven days a week.
77.   **toward:** in preparation.
78.   **Doth ... day:** keeps day and night shifts working.
83.   **pricked ... pride:** urged on by ambitious pride.
87.   **heraldry:** codes of chivalry.

Which he stood seized of,° to the conqueror;
Against the which a moiety competent° 90
Was gaged° by our King; which had returned°
To the inheritance of Fortinbras,
Had he been vanquisher, as, by the same cov'nant
And carriage of the article designed,°
His fell to Hamlet.° Now, sir, young Fortinbras, 95
Of unimproved mettle hot and full,
Hath in the skirts° of Norway, here and there,
Sharked up° a list of lawless resolutes,°
For food and diet° to some enterprise
That hath a stomach in't;° which is no other, 100
As it doth well appear unto our state,
But to recover of us, by strong hand
And terms compulsatory,° those foresaid lands
So by his father lost; and this, I take it,
Is the main motive of our preparations, 105
The source of this our watch, and the chief head°
Of this post-haste and romage° in the land.

Bernardo.

I think it be no other but e'en so.°
Well may it sort° that this portentous figure

---

89.   **stood seized of:** possessed.
90.   **moiety competent:** sufficient portion.
91.   **gaged:** pledged. **had returned:** would have returned.
94.   **carriage ... designed:** fulfillment of the clause in the agreement.
86–95. **who ... Hamlet:** There was a formal agreement (the "sealed
      compact") that the victor wins the loser's lands.
97.   **skirts:** outskirts.
98.   **sharked up:** snatched. **resolutes:** desperadoes.
99.   **For ... diet:** as cannon fodder.
100. **hath ... in't:** requires.
103. **terms compulsatory:** force.
106. **head:** source.
107. **post-haste and romage:** furious activity and turmoil.
108. **e'en so:** exactly so.
109. **Well ... sort:** It would be fitting.

Comes armed through our watch, so like the King   110
That was and is the question° of these wars.

Horatio.

A mote° it is to trouble the mind's eye.
In the most high and palmy° state of Rome,
A little ere the mightiest Julius fell,
The graves stood tenantless, and the sheeted° dead   115
Did squeak° and gibber in the Roman streets;
As° stars with trains of fire, and dews of blood,
Disasters in the sun; and the moist star
Upon whose influence Neptune's empire stands°
Was sick almost to doomsday with eclipse.   120
And even the like precurse° of fierce events,
As harbingers° preceding still the fates
And prologue to the omen coming on,
Have heaven and earth together demonstrated
Unto our climatures° and countrymen.   125

Re-enter GHOST.

But soft! behold! Lo, where it comes again!
I'll cross it,° though it blast me. —Stay, illusion!
If thou hast any sound, or use of voice,
Speak to me.
If there be any good thing to be done,   130
That may to thee do ease, and grace to me,
Speak to me.
If thou art privy to thy country's fate,

---

111. **question:** occasion.
112. **mote:** speck of dust.
113. **palmy:** flourishing.
115. **sheeted:** shrouded.
116. **squeak:** Ghosts were believed to have shrill voices.
117. **As:** Probably a line of the play is missing here.
118–19. **the moist … stands:** the moon, which controls the tides.
121. **even … precurse:** exactly the same forewarning.
122. **harbingers:** forerunners.
125. **climatures:** regions.
127. **cross it:** cross its path.

Which, happily, foreknowing may avoid,
O, speak! 135
Or if thou hast uphoarded in thy life
Extorted° treasure in the womb of earth
(For which, they say, you spirits oft walk in death),

The cock crows.

Speak of it!° Stay, and speak! —Stop it, Marcellus!
Marcellus.
Shall I strike at it with my partisan?° 140
Horatio.
Do, if it will not stand.
Bernardo.　　　　　　　'Tis here!
Horatio.　　　　　　　　　　'Tis here!
Marcellus.
'Tis gone!

　　　　　　　　　　　　　　　　　Exit GHOST.

We do it wrong, being so majestical,
To offer it the show of violence;
For it is, as the air, invulnerable, 145
And our vain blows malicious mockery.
Bernardo.
It was about to speak, when the cock crew.
Horatio.
And then it started, like a guilty thing
Upon a fearful summons. I have heard
The cock, that is the trumpet to the morn, 150
Doth with his lofty and shrill-sounding throat
Awake the god of day; and, at his warning,
Whether in sea or fire, in earth or air,

128–39. **If … Speak of it!:** There were four reasons why a ghost might
　　　walk: to reveal a secret, to utter a warning, to reveal concealed treas-
　　　ure, to reveal the manner of its death. Horatio uses three of these
　　　reasons, but before he can say the fourth, the cock crows.
137. **Extorted:** ill won.
140. **partisan:** long-handled spear.

The extravagant and erring spirit hies
To his confine;° and of the truth herein   155
This present object made probation.°

Marcellus.

It faded on the crowing of the cock.
Some say that ever 'gainst that season comes°
Wherein our Savior's birth is celebrated,
The bird of dawning° singeth all night long;   160
And then, they say, no spirit dares stir abroad,
The nights are wholesome, then no planets strike,°
No fairy takes, nor witch hath power to charm,
So hallowed and so gracious° is the time.

Horatio.

So have I heard and do in part believe it.   165
But look, the morn, in russet° mantle clad,
Walks o'er the dew of yon high eastern hill.
Break we our watch up; and by my advice
Let us impart what we have seen tonight
Unto young Hamlet; for, upon my life,   170
This spirit, dumb to us, will speak to him.
Do you consent we shall acquaint him with it,
As needful in our loves,° fitting our duty?

Marcellus.

Let's do't, I pray; and I this morning know
Where we shall find him most conveniently.   175

Exeunt.

154–55. The ... confine: The wandering ghost hastens to its place of
    confinement.
156.   probation: proof.
158.   'gainst ... comes: in anticipation of that time.
160.   bird of dawning: rooster.
162.   strike: destroy (by means of evil influence).
164.   gracious: blessed.
166.   russet: reddish brown.
173.   As ... loves: as our love for him requires.

Scene 2. *A room of state in the castle.*

Enter KING CLAUDIUS, QUEEN GERTRUDE, HAMLET, POLONIUS,
LAERTES, VOLTEMAND, CORNELIUS, LORDS, *and* ATTENDANTS.

King.
> Though yet of Hamlet our° dear brother's death
> The memory be green, and that it us befitted
> To bear our hearts in grief, and our whole kingdom
> To be contracted in one brow of woe,
> Yet so far hath discretion fought with nature°   5
> That we with wisest sorrow think on him
> Together with remembrance of ourselves.
> Therefore our sometime sister,° now our queen,
> The imperial jointress° to this warlike state,
> Have we, as 'twere with a defeated joy,   10
> With an auspicious, and a dropping eye,°
> With mirth in funeral, and with dirge in marriage,
> In equal scale weighing delight and dole,°
> Taken to wife; nor have we herein barred
> Your better wisdoms,° which have freely gone   15
> With this affair along. For all, our thanks.
> Now follows, that you know, young Fortinbras,
> Holding a weak supposal of our worth,°
> Or thinking by our late dear brother's death
> Our state to be disjoint and out of frame,°   20
> Colleagued with this dream of his advantage,°

I.2.1. **our:** my. (Claudius refers to himself with the royal *we.*)
5. **hath ... nature:** Common sense has won out over natural feelings of sorrow.
8. **our ... sister:** my former sister-in-law.
9. **jointress:** joint holder.
11. **With ... eye:** joyful and tearful simultaneously.
13. **dole:** grief.
14–15. **nor ... wisdoms:** nor have I ignored your advice.
18. **weak ... worth:** low opinion of my ability.
20. **disjoint ... frame:** at loose ends and out of control.
20–21. **Colleagued ... advantage:** allied with the illusion of his success.

He hath not failed to pester us with message
Importing the surrender of those lands
Lost by his father, with all bands of law,°
To our most valiant brother. So much for him.   25
Now for ourself and for° this time of meeting.
Thus much the business is: we have here writ
To Norway, uncle of young Fortinbras,
Who, impotent and bedrid, scarcely hears
Of this his nephew's purpose, to suppress   30
His further gait° herein, in that° the levies,
The lists, and full proportions are all made
Out of his subject; ° and we here dispatch
You, good Cornelius, and you, Voltemand,
For bearers of this greeting to old Norway,   35
Giving to you no further personal power
To business° with the King, more than the scope°
Of these dilated articles° allow.

Gives a paper.

Farewell, and let your haste commend your duty.°
Cornelius and Voltemand.
In that, and all things, will we show our duty.   40
King.
We doubt it nothing. Heartily farewell.

Exeunt VOLTEMAND *and* CORNELIUS.

And now, Laertes, what's the news with you?
You told us of some suit.° What is't, Laertes?

23–24. **Importing ... law:** dealing with the legally binding agreement
      between the two kings.
26.   **and for:** and the reason for.
31.   **gait:** progress. **in that:** based on the fact that.
32–33. **The ... subject:** The lists of recruits are made up of his
      subjects.
37.   **To business:** to do business. **scope:** limit.
38.   **dilated articles:** detailed accounts.
39.   **let ... duty:** be quick to do your duty.
43.   **suit:** petition.

You cannot speak of reason to the Dane°
And lose your voice.° What wouldst thou° beg,
    Laertes,   45
That shall not be my offer, not thy asking?
The head is not more native° to the heart,
The hand more instrumental° to the mouth,
Than is the throne of Denmark to thy father.
What wouldst thou have, Laertes?

Laertes.   My dread° lord,   50
Your leave and favor° to return to France,
From whence though willingly I came to Denmark
To show my duty in your coronation,
Yet now I must confess, that duty done,
My thoughts and wishes bend again toward France   55
And bow them to your gracious leave and pardon.

King.
Have you your father's leave? What says Polonius?

Polonius.
He hath, my lord, wrung from me my slow leave
By laborsome petition, and at last
Upon his will I sealed my hard consent.°   60
I do beseech you give him leave to go.

King.
Take thy fair hour,° Laertes. Time be thine,
And thy best graces spend it at thy will!
But now, my cousin° Hamlet, and my son—

Hamlet. [*Aside.*]
A little more than kin, and less than kind!°   65

---

44.   **the Dane:** the king.
45.   **lose ... voice:** waste your breath. **thou:** the familiar form of *you.*
47.   **native:** closely related.
48.   **instrumental:** useful.
50.   **dread:** respected.
51.   **leave and favor:** permission and approval.
60.   **will ... consent:** Since he desired it, I reluctantly agreed.
62.   **Take ... hour:** Make the most of your youth.
64.   **cousin:** kinsman
65.   **more ... kind:** more than kinsmen (uncle-nephew and stepfather-stepson) but not similar in nature.

King.
　　How is it that the clouds still hang on you?
Hamlet.
　　Not so, my lord. I am too much i' the sun.°
Queen.
　　Good Hamlet, cast thy nighted° color off,
　　And let thine eye look like a friend on Denmark.
　　Do not for ever with thy vailèd lids°　　　　　　70°
　　Seek for thy noble father in the dust.
　　Thou know'st 'tis common,° all that lives must die,
　　Passing through nature to eternity.
Hamlet.
　　Ay, madam, it is common.
Queen.　　　　　　　　　　　If it be,
　　Why seems it so particular with thee?°　　　　　75
Hamlet.
　　Seems, madam? Nay, it is. I know not "seems."
　　'Tis not alone my inky cloak, good mother,
　　Nor customary suits of solemn black,
　　Nor windy suspiration° of forced breath,
　　No, nor the fruitful river in the eye,°　　　　　80
　　Nor the dejected havior of the visage,°
　　Together with all forms, moods, shapes of grief,
　　That can denote me truly. These indeed seem,
　　For they are actions that a man might play;°
　　But I have that within which passeth show—　　85
　　These but the trappings° and the suits of woe.
King.
　　'Tis sweet and commendable in your nature, Hamlet,

67.　**sun:** pun on *son, sun.*
68.　**nighted:** dark. (Hamlet is dressed in black.)
70.　**vailèd lids:** lowered eyelids.
72.　**common:** universally true.
75.　**Why ... thee?:** Why do you act as if death affected only you?
79.　**windy suspiration:** deep sighing.
80.　**fruitful ... eye:** heavy weeping.
81.　**dejected ... visage:** sad facial expression.
84.　**play:** playact.
86.　**trappings:** ornaments.

To give these mourning duties to your father;
But you must know, your father lost a father;
That father lost, lost his, and the survivor bound   90
In filial obligation for some term
To do obsequious° sorrow. But to persever°
In obstinate condolement° is a course
Of impious stubbornness. 'Tis unmanly grief;
It shows a will most incorrect to heaven,°   95
A heart unfortified, a mind impatient,
An understanding simple and unschooled;
For what we know must be, and is as common
As any the most vulgar thing to sense,°
Why should we in our peevish° opposition   100
Take it to heart? Fie! 'tis a fault to heaven,
A fault against the dead, a fault to nature,
To reason most absurd, whose common theme
Is death of fathers, and who still° hath cried,
From the first corse° till he that died today,   105
"This must be so." We pray you throw to earth
This unprevailing° woe, and think of us
As of a father; for let the world take note
You are the most immediate° to our throne,
And with no less nobility of love   110
Than that which dearest father bears his son
Do I impart toward you. For your intent
In going back to school in Wittenberg,
It is most retrograde° to our desire;
And we beseech you, bend you° to remain   115

---

92. **obsequious:** appropriate to funeral rites. **persever:** persevere.
93. **condolement:** grief.
95. **incorrect to heaven:** not submissive to divine will.
99. **any ... sense:** that which is most familiar to common observation.
100. **peevish:** foolish.
104. **still:** always.
105. **corse:** corpse.
107. **unprevailing:** futile.
109. **most immediate:** next in line.
114. **retrograde:** contrary.
115. **bend you:** submit yourself.

Here in the cheer and comfort of our eye,
Our chiefest courtier, cousin, and our son.

Queen.

Let not thy mother lose her prayers, Hamlet:
I pray thee, stay with us, go not to Wittenberg.

Hamlet.

I shall in all my best° obey you, madam.   120

King.

Why, 'tis a loving and a fair reply.
Be as ourself° in Denmark. Madam, come.
This gentle and unforced accord of Hamlet
Sits smiling to my heart; in grace whereof,°
No jocund health that Denmark° drinks today   125
But the great cannon to the clouds shall tell,
And the King's rouse the heavens all bruit° again,
Respeaking earthly thunder. Come away.

> *Flourish. Exeunt all but* HAMLET.

Hamlet.

O, that this too too solid flesh would melt,
Thaw, and resolve itself into a dew!   130
Or that the Everlasting had not fixed
His canon° 'gainst self-slaughter! O God! God!
How weary, stale, flat, and unprofitable
Seem to me all the uses of this world!
Fie on't! ah, fie! 'Tis an unweeded garden   135
That grows to seed; things rank and gross in nature
Possess it merely.° That it should come to this!

---

120. **in ... best:** to the best of my ability.
122. **Be ... ourself:** Use all the king's privileges.
124. **in grace whereof:** in honor of which.
125. **No ... Denmark:** no merry toast that the king.
126–27. **cannon ... bruit:** According to Danish custom, a cannon was fired
    when the king proposed a toast. The cannon's thunder would cause
    the toast to echo from the skies.
132. **canon:** law.
137. **merely:** entirely.

But two months dead—nay, not so much, not two!
So excellent a king, that was to this
Hyperion to a satyr;° so loving to my mother 140
That he might not beteem° the winds of heaven
Visit her face too roughly. Heaven and earth!
Must I remember? Why, she would hang on him
As if increase of appetite had grown
By what it fed on; and yet, within a month— 145
Let me not think on't. Frailty, thy name is woman!—
A little month, or ere° those shoes were old
With which she followed my poor father's body,
Like Niobe,° all tears—why she, even she—
O God! a beast, that wants° discourse of reason 150
Would have mourned longer—married with my uncle;
My father's brother, but no more like my father
Than I to Hercules.° Within a month,
Ere yet the salt of most unrighteous° tears
Had left the flushing in her galled eyes, 155
She married. O, most wicked speed, to post°
With such dexterity° to incestuous° sheets!
It is not, nor it cannot come to good.
But break my heart, for I must hold my tongue!

Enter HORATIO, MARCELLUS, *and* BERNARDO.

Horatio.
Hail to your lordship!

139–40. **So ... satyr:** Hamlet's father was like Hyperion (the handsome
    sun god) compared to Claudius, whom Hamlet sees as a satyr (a
    goatlike, lustful mythological creature).
141. **beteem:** allow.
147. **ere:** before.
149. **Niobe:** in Greek legend, a woman who wept ceaselessly when her
    children were slain by Apollo.
150. **wants:** lacks the ability to.
153. **Hercules:** a Greek hero who performed superhuman tasks.
154. **unrighteous:** insincere.
156. **post:** hasten.
157. **dexterity:** nimbleness. **incestuous:** referring here to Gertrude's mar-
    rying her husband's brother.

Hamlet. I am glad to see you well.   160
   Horatio—or I do forget myself!
Horatio.
   The same, my lord, and your poor servant ever.
Hamlet.
   Sir, my good friend—I'll change that name with you.°
   And what make you from Wittenberg, Horatio?
   Marcellus?   165
Marcellus. My good lord!
Hamlet.
   I am very glad to see you. [*To* BERNARDO.] Good
      even,° sir.
   But what, in faith, make you from Wittenberg?
Horatio.
   A truant disposition,° good my lord.
Hamlet.
   I would not hear your enemy say so,   170
   Nor shall you do mine ear that violence
   To make it truster° of your own report
   Against yourself. I know you are no truant.
   But what is your affair in Elsinore?
   We'll teach you to drink deep ere you depart.   175
Horatio.
   My lord, I came to see your father's funeral.
Hamlet.
   I prithee, do not mock me, fellow student,
   I think it was to see my mother's wedding.
Horatio.
   Indeed, my lord, it followed hard upon.°

---

163. **change ... you:** exchange the title of friend (so that they may be
      friends and equals).
167. **Good even:** Good evening (a greeting used any time after noon).
169. **disposition:** whim, mood.
172. **truster:** believer.
179. **hard upon:** soon after.

Hamlet.

    Thrift, thrift, Horatio! The funeral baked meats   180

    Did coldly furnish forth the marriage tables.°

    Would I had met my dearest° foe in heaven

    Or ever I had seen that day, Horatio!

    My father!—methinks I see my father.

Horatio.

    O, where, my lord?

Hamlet.   In my mind's eye, Horatio.   185

Horatio.

    I saw him once. He was a goodly king.

Hamlet.

    He was a man, take him for all in all.

    I shall not look upon his like again.

Horatio.

    My lord, I think I saw him yesternight.

Hamlet. Saw? who?   190

Horatio.

    My lord, the King your father.

Hamlet.   The King my father?

Horatio.

    Season your admiration° for a while

    With an attent° ear, till I may deliver,

    Upon the witness of these gentlemen,

    This marvel to you.

Hamlet.   For God's love, let me hear!   195

Horatio.

    Two nights together had these gentlemen,

    Marcellus and Bernardo, on their watch

    In the dead vast° and middle of the night

180–81. **Thrift … tables:** The marriage came so soon after the king's
    funeral that the hot food left over from the funeral could thriftily
    be served cold at the wedding reception.

182.   **dearest:** most hated.

192.   **Season your admiration:** Moderate your astonishment.

193.   **attent:** attentive.

198:   **vast:** emptiness.

Been thus encount'red. A figure like your father,
Armed at point exactly, cap-a-pe,° 200
Appears before them and with solemn march
Goes slow and stately by them. Thrice he walked
By their oppressed and fear-surprised eyes,
Within his truncheon's° length; whilst they, distilled°
Almost to jelly with the act of fear, 205
Stand dumb and speak not to him. This to me
In dreadful° secrecy impart they did,
And I with them the third night kept the watch;
Where, as they had delivered, both in time,
Form° of the thing, each word made true and good, 210
The apparition comes. I knew your father:
These hands are not more like.°

Hamlet. But where was this?
Marcellus.

My lord, upon the platform where we watched.
Hamlet.

Did you not speak to it?
Horatio. My lord, I did;
But answer made it none. Yet once methought 215
It lifted up its head and did address
Itself to motion, like as it would speak;
But even° then the morning cock crew loud,
And at the sound it shrunk in haste away
And vanished from our sight.
Hamlet. 'Tis very strange. 220
Horatio.

As I do live, my honored lord, 'tis true;
And we did think it writ down in our duty

---

200. **at ... cap-a-pe:** correctly and in every detail from head to foot.
204. **truncheon:** staff (a symbol of authority). **distilled:** dissolved.
207. **dreadful:** terrified.
210. **Form:** appearance.
212. **These ...like:** These hands of mine as much alike as Hamlet's father
and the Ghost.
218. **even:** just.

To let you know of it.
Hamlet.
Indeed, indeed, sirs, but this troubles me.
Hold you the watch tonight?
Marcellus and Bernardo.   We do, my lord.   225
Hamlet. Armed, say you?
Marcellus and Bernardo. Armed, my lord.
Hamlet.
From top to toe?
Marcellus and Bernardo. My lord, from head to foot.
Hamlet. ·
Then saw you not his face?
Horatio.
O, yes, my lord! He wore his beaver° up.   230
Hamlet.
What, looked he frowningly?
Horatio.
A countenance more in sorrow than in anger.
Hamlet. Pale or red?
Horatio.
Nay, very pale.
Hamlet.   And fixed his eyes upon you?
Horatio.
Most constantly.
Hamlet.   I would I had been there.   235
Horatio.
It would have much amazed you.
Hamlet.
Very like, very like.° Stayed it long?
Horatio.
While one with moderate haste might tell° a hundred.
Marcellus and Bernardo. Longer, longer.

---

230. **beaver:** visor (face guard).
237. **Very like:** most likely.
238. **tell:** count.

Horatio.

Not when I saw't.

Hamlet.　　　　　　His beard was grizzled°—no?　　　240

Horatio.

It was, as I have seen it in his life,
A sable silvered.°

Hamlet.　　　　　I will watch tonight.

Perchance 'twill walk again.

Horatio.　　　　　　I warr'nt it will.

Hamlet.

If it assume my noble father's person,
I'll speak to it, though hell itself should gape°　　　245
And bid me hold my peace. I pray you all,
If you have hitherto concealed this sight,
Let it be tenable° in your silence still;
And whatsoever else shall hap tonight,
Give it an understanding but no tongue.　　　250
I will requite° your loves. So, fare you well.
Upon the platform, 'twixt eleven and twelve,
I'll visit you.

Marcellus, Bernardo, and Horatio. Our duty to your honor.

Hamlet.

Your loves, as mine to you. Farewell.

Exeunt all but HAMLET.

My father's spirit—in arms? All is not well.　　　255
I doubt° some foul play.° Would the night were come!
Till then sit still, my soul. Foul deeds will rise,

---

240. **grizzled:** gray or with gray in it.
242. **A sable silvered:** black mixed with white.
245. **gape:** open. (Hamlet is aware that the Ghost might be a demon and not his father's spirit.)
248. **tenable:** held fast.
251. **requite:** repay.
256. **doubt:** fear. **foul play:** People believed that one reason a ghost appeared was to disclose a crime.

Though all the earth o'erwhelm them, to men's eyes.

Exit.

Scene 3. *A room in Polonius' house.*

Enter LAERTES *and* OPHELIA.

Laertes.
My necessaries° are embarked. Farewell.
And, sister, as the winds give benefit
And convoy is assistant, do not sleep,
But let me hear from you.°
Ophelia.   Do you doubt that?
Laertes.
For Hamlet, and the trifling of his favor,   5
Hold it a fashion and a toy in blood;°
A violet in the youth of primy nature,
Forward,° not permanent— sweet, not lasting;
The perfume and suppliance° of a minute;
No more.
Ophelia.   No more but so?°
Laertes.   Think it no more.   10
For nature crescent does not grow alone
In thews and bulk,° but as this temple waxes,°
The inward service of the mind and soul
Grows wide withal.° Perhaps he loves you now,

I.3.1. **necessaries:** baggage.
2–4.   **as ... you:** Whenever ships (that carry mail) set sail, please write
         to me.
6.   **a fashion ... blood:** a fad and a whim of his impetuous nature.
8.   **Forward:** blooming early.
9.   **suppliance:** pastime.
10.   **No ... so?:** Nothing more than that?
11–12. **For ... bulk:** For natural growth is not only in bodily bulk. **temple
         waxes:** body grows.
14.   **withal:** at the same time.

And now no soil nor cautel° doth besmirch   15
The virtue of his will;° but you must fear,
His greatness weighed,° his will is not his own,
For he himself is subject to his birth.
He may not, as unvalued° persons do,
Carve° for himself, for on his choice depends   20
The safety and health of this whole state,
And therefore must his choice be circumscribed°
Unto the voice and yielding of that body°
Whereof he is the head. Then if he says he loves you,
It fits your wisdom so far to believe it   25
As he in his particular act and place
May give his saying deed,° which is no further
Than the main voice of Denmark goes withal.
Then weigh what loss your honor may sustain
If with too credent° ear you list his songs,°   30
Or lose your heart, or your chaste treasure open
To his unmast'red importunity.°
Fear it, Ophelia, fear it, my dear sister,
And keep you in the rear of your affection,°
Out of the shot and danger of desire.   35
The chariest maid is prodigal° enough
If she unmask her beauty to the moon.
Virtue itself scapes not calumnious strokes.
The canker galls the infants of the spring
Too oft before their buttons be disclosed,°   40

---

15. **cautel:** deceit.
16. **will:** desire.
17. **His ... weighed:** if his noble birth is considered.
19. **unvalued:** of low rank.
20. **Carve:** choose.
22. **circumscribed:** restricted.
23. **yielding ... body:** the consent of the Danish state.
27. **give ... deed:** act upon his words of love.
30. **credent:** believing. **list:** listen to.
32. **unmast'red importunity:** uncontrolled pleas.
34. **keep ... affection:** stay out of the range of temptation.
36. **The ... prodigal:** The most modest maiden is reckless.
39–40. **The canker ... disclosed:** The cankerworm kills the earliest buds.

And in the morn and liquid dew of youth
Contagious blastments° are most imminent.
Be wary then; best safety lies in fear.
Youth to itself rebels, though none else near.
Ophelia.
 I shall the effect of this good lesson keep   45
 As watchman to my heart. But, good my brother,
 Do not, as some ungracious° pastors do,
 Show me the steep and thorny way to heaven,
 Whiles, like a puffed° and reckless libertine,
 Himself the primrose path of dalliance treads 50
 And recks not his own rede.°
Laertes.   O, fear me not!
 I stay too long. But here my father comes.

Enter POLONIUS.

 A double blessing is a double grace;
 Occasion smiles upon a second leave.°
Polonius.
 Yet here, Laertes? Aboard, aboard, for shame! 55
 The wind sits in the shoulder of your sail,
 And you are stayed° for. There—my blessing with thee!
 And these few precepts in thy memory
 Look thou character. Give thy thoughts no tongue,
 Nor any unproportioned° thought his act.   60
 Be thou familiar, but by no means vulgar:°
 Those friends thou hast, and their adoption tried,°

---

42. **contagious blastments:** infectious blights (*Blasting* is a withering disease of plants. This continues the flower metaphor from line 39.)
47. **ungracious:** ungodly.
49. **puffed:** swollen.
50–51. **Himself ... rede:** Do not be like the one who is tempted (to flirt) and does not follow his own advice.
53–54. **A double ... leave:** Fortune is smiling, for she gives me two farewell blessings.
57. **stayed:** waited.
60. **unproportioned:** undisciplined.
61. **vulgar:** easily accessible (to friendship).
62. **adoption tried:** friendship tested.

Grapple them to thy soul with hoops of steel;
But do not dull thy palm with entertainment
Of each new-hatched, unfledged comrade. Beware   65
Of entrance to a quarrel; but being in,
Bear't that the opposed may beware of thee.
Give every man thy ear, but few thy voice;
Take each man's censure,° but reserve thy judgment.
Costly thy habit° as thy purse can buy,   70
But not expressed in fancy;° rich, not gaudy;
For the apparel oft proclaims the man,
And they in France of the best rank and station
Are of a most select and generous, chief in that.°
Neither a borrower nor a lender be;   75
For loan oft loses both itself and friend,
And borrowing dulls the edge of husbandry.°
This above all: to thine ownself be true,
And it must follow, as the night the day,
Thou canst not then be false to any man.   80
Farewell. My blessing season° this in thee!

Laertes.
Most humbly do I take my leave, my lord.

Polonius.
The time invites you. Go, your servants tend.°

Laertes.
Farewell, Ophelia, and remember well
What I have said to you.

Ophelia.   'Tis in my memory locked,   85
And you yourself shall keep the key of it.°

---

69.   **censure:** opinion.
70.   **habit:** clothing.
71.   **fancy:** ornamentation.
73–74. **they … that:** and Frenchmen of the highest rank are distinguished
       by their understated clothes.
77.   **husbandry:** thrift.
81.   **season:** ripen, mature.
83.   **tend:** are waiting.
85–86. **'Tis … it:** I will remember it until you permit me to forget it.

Laertes. Farewell.

Exit.

Polonius.
What is't, Ophelia, he hath said to you?
Ophelia.
So please you, something touching the Lord Hamlet.
Polonius.
Marry,° well bethought!° 90
'Tis told me, he hath very oft of late
Given private time to you, and you yourself
Have of your audience been most free° and bounteous.
If it be so—as so 'tis put on me,
And that in way of caution°— I must tell you 95
You do not understand yourself so clearly
As it behooves° my daughter and your honor.
What is between you? Give me up the truth.
Ophelia.
He hath, my lord, of late made many tenders°
Of his affection to me. 100
Polonius.
Affection? Pooh! You speak like a green° girl,
Unsifted in such perilous circumstance.
Do you believe his tenders, as you call them?
Ophelia.
I do not know, my lord, what I should think.
Polonius.
Marry, I will teach you! Think yourself a baby 105
That you have ta'en these tenders for true pay,
Which are not sterling.° Tender° yourself more dearly,

---

90. **Marry:** a mild oath. **bethought:** remembered.
93. **free:** liberal.
94–95. **as ... caution:** as people have been warning me.
97. **behooves:** is the duty of.
99. **tenders:** offers.
101. **green:** inexperienced.
107. **sterling:** real money. **Tender:** Value.

Or (not to crack the wind of the poor phrase,
Running it thus) you'll tender me a fool.°

Ophelia.

My lord, he hath importuned me with love   110
In honorable fashion.

Polonius. Ay, fashion° you may call it. Go to, go to!°

Ophelia.

And hath given countenance to his speech, my lord,
With almost all the holy vows of heaven.

Polonius.

Ay, springes° to catch woodcocks! I do know,   115
When the blood burns, how prodigal° the soul
Lends the tongue vows. These blazes,° daughter,
Giving more light than heat, extinct in both
Even in their promise, as it is a-making,°
You must not take for fire. From this time   120
Be somewhat scanter of your maiden presence.
Set your entreatments at a higher rate
Than a command to parley.° For Lord Hamlet,
Believe so much in him, that he is young,
And with a larger tether° may he walk   125
Than may be given you. In few,° Ophelia,
Do not believe his vows; for they are brokers,°
Not of that dye which their investments° show,
But mere implorators of unholy suits,

---

109. **tender ... fool:** make me appear foolish; produce a grandchild.
112. **fashion:** mere show. **Go to, go to:** Come, come.
115. **springes:** traps.
116. **prodigal:** extravagantly.
117. **blazes:** sudden flashes.
118–19. **extinct ... a-making:** their heat and light dying out as soon as they are formed.
122–23. **Set ... parley:** The imagery is that of courtship as a battle. It can be paraphrased as "Play hard to get."
125. **larger tether:** longer rope. (Hamlet is freer than Ophelia.)
126. **In few:** in short.
127. **brokers:** panderers.
128. **investments:** clothing.

Breathing like sanctified and pious bawds,°   130
The better to beguile. This is for all:
I would not, in plain terms, from this time forth
Have you so slander any moment leisure°
As to give words or talk with the Lord Hamlet.
Look to't, I charge you. Come your ways.   135
Ophelia.
    I shall obey, my lord.

Exeunt.

Scene 4. *The platform.*

Enter HAMLET, HORATIO, *and* MARCELLUS.

Hamlet.
    The air bites shrewdly;° it is very cold.
Horatio.
    It is a nipping and an eager° air.
Hamlet.
    What hour now?
Horatio.   I think it lacks of twelve.
Marcellus.
    No, it is struck.
Horatio.
    Indeed? I heard it not. Then it draws near the season   5
    Wherein the spirit held his wont° to walk.

A flourish of trumpets, and ordnance shot off, within.

    What does this mean, my lord?

---

130.   **Breathing ... bawds:** acting piously to hide their real purpose as procurers.
133.   **slander ... leisure:** misuse any spare moment.
I.4.1. **shrewdly:** keenly.
2.   **eager:** sharp.
6.   **held his wont:** was accustomed.

Hamlet.
 The King doth wake tonight and takes his rouse,
 Keeps wassail, and the swagg'ring upspring reels,
 And, as he drains his draughts of Rhenish down,°   10
 The kettledrum and trumpet thus bray out
 The triumph of his pledge.°
Horatio.   Is it a custom?
Hamlet.
 Ay, marry, is't;
 But to my mind, though I am native here
 And to the manner born, it is a custom   15
 More honored in the breach than the observance.°
 This heavy-headed revel east and west
 Makes us traduced and taxed of° other nations;
 They clepe° us drunkards and with swinish phrase
 Soil our addition;° and indeed it takes   20
 From our achievements, though performed at height,
 The pith and marrow of our attribute.
 So oft it chances in particular men°
 That for some vicious mole° of nature in them,
 As in their birth—wherein they are not guilty,   25
 Since nature cannot choose his origin—
 By their o'ergrowth of some complexion,°
 Oft breaking down the pales° and forts of reason,
 Or by some habit that too much o'erleavens
 The form of plausive manners,° that these men   30
 Carrying, I say, the stamp of one defect,

8–10. **doth … down:** stays up late and carouses, revels, and dances wildly
   as he swills down Rhine wine.
12. **pledge:** toast to one's health.
16. **More … observance:** more honorable to neglect than to observe.
18. **taxed of:** censured by.
19. **clepe:** call.
20. **soil our addition:** besmirch our good name.
23. **particular men:** some individuals.
24. **mole:** blemish.
27. **o'ergrowth … complexion:** excess of humors.
28. **pales:** fences.
29–30. **o'erleavens … manners:** corrupts the pattern of approved behavior.

Being nature's livery, or fortune's star,°
Their virtues else—be they as pure as grace,
As infinite as man may undergo—
Shall in the general censure° take corruption   35
From that particular fault. The dram of e'il
Doth all the noble substance often doubt
To his own scandal.°

Enter GHOST.

Horatio.   Look, my lord, it comes!
Hamlet.
Angels and ministers° of grace defend us!
Be thou a spirit of health° or goblin damned,   40
Bring with thee airs from heaven or blasts from hell,
Be thy intents wicked or charitable,
Thou com'st in such a questionable° shape
That I will speak to thee. I'll call thee Hamlet,
King, father, royal Dane. O, answer me!   45
Let me not burst in ignorance, but tell
Why thy canonized° bones, hearsed in death,°
Have burst their cerements;° why the sepulcher
Wherein we saw thee quietly inurned,°
Hath oped his ponderous and marble jaws   50
To cast thee up again. What may this mean
That thou, dead corse, again in complete steel,
Revisits thus the glimpses of the moon,°
Making night hideous, and we fools of nature

---

32. **nature's ... star:** inborn or from bad luck.
35. **general censure:** public opinion.
36–38. **The dram ... scandal:** The little drop of evil often blots out the noble
      substance, bringing scandal to it.
39. **ministers:** messengers of God.
40. **spirit of health:** a good angel.
43. **questionable:** inviting questioning.
47. **canonized:** having been given the sacred rites of burial. **hearsed in
      death:** put in a coffin.
48. **cerements:** burial clothes.
49. **inurned:** entombed.
53. **glimpses of the moon:** fitful moonlight.

So horridly to shake our disposition°   55
With thoughts beyond the reaches of our souls?
Say, why is this? wherefore? What should we do?

GHOST *beckons* HAMLET.

Horatio.
It beckons you to go away with it,
As if it some impartment° did desire
To you alone.
Marcellus.   Look with what courteous action   60
It waves you to a more removed ground.
But do not go with it!
Horatio.   No, by no means!
Hamlet.
It will not speak. Then I will follow it.
Horatio.
Do not, my lord!
Hamlet.   Why, what should be the fear?
I do not set my life at a pin's fee;°   65
And for my soul, what can it do to that,
Being a thing immortal as itself?
It waves me forth again. I'll follow it.
Horatio.
What if it tempt you toward the flood, my lord,
Or to the dreadful summit of the cliff   70
That beetles o'er° his base into the sea,
And there assume some other, horrible form
Which might deprive your sovereignty° of reason
And draw you into madness? Think of it.
The very place puts toys° of desperation,   75
Without more motive, into every brain

---

55. **disposition:** mental constitution.
59. **impartment:** disclosure.
65. **fee:** value.
71. **beetles o'er:** overhangs.
73. **sovereignty:** power.
75. **toys:** irrational impulses.

That looks so many fathoms to the sea
And hears it roar beneath.
Hamlet.   It waves me still.
Go on, I'll follow thee.
Marcellus.
You shall not go, my lord.
Hamlet.   Hold off your hands!   80
Horatio.
Be ruled, you shall not go.
Hamlet.   My fate cries out
And makes each petty artery in this body
As hardy as the Nemean lion's° nerve.

GHOST *beckons.*

Still am I called. Unhand me, gentlemen—
By heaven, I'll make a ghost of him that lets° me!   85
I say, away!—Go on, I'll follow thee.

Exeunt GHOST *and* HAMLET.

Horatio.
He waxes desperate with imagination.
Marcellus.
Let's follow; 'tis not fit thus to obey him.
Horatio.
Have after.° To what issue will this come?
Marcellus.
Something is rotten in the state of Denmark.   90
Horatio.
Heaven will direct it.°
Marcellus.   Nay, let's follow him.

Exeunt.

---

83.   **Nemean lion:** beast slain by Hercules.
85.   **lets:** hinders.
89.   **Have after:** Let's pursue.
91.   **it:** The word *it* refers to *issue* (line 89).

Scene 5. *Another part of the platform.*

Enter GHOST *and* HAMLET.

Hamlet.
Where wilt thou lead me? Speak, I'll go no further.
Ghost.
Mark me.
Hamlet.   I will.
Ghost.   My hour is almost come,
When I to sulph'rous and tormenting flames
Must render up myself.°
Hamlet.   Alas, poor ghost!
Ghost.
Pity me not, but lend thy serious hearing   5
To what I shall unfold.
Hamlet.   Speak, I am bound to hear.
Ghost.
So art thou to revenge, when thou shalt hear.
Hamlet. What?
Ghost.
I am thy father's spirit,
Doomed for a certain term to walk the night,   10
And for the day confined to fast in fires,
Till the foul crimes° done in my days of nature
Are burnt and purged away. But that I am forbid
To tell the secrets of my prison house,
I could a tale unfold whose lightest word   15
Would harrow up thy soul, freeze thy young blood,
Make thy two eyes, like stars, start from their spheres,
Thy knotted and combined locks° to part,
And each particular hair to stand on end

I.5.2–4. **My ... myself:** At daybreak, the Ghost must return to purgatory
(see lines 11–13).
12.   **crimes:** sins.
18.   **combined locks:** neatly arranged hair.

Like quills upon the fretful porpentine.°   20
But this eternal blazon° must not be
To ears of flesh and blood. List, list, O, list!
If thou didst ever thy dear father love—
Hamlet. O God!
Ghost.
Revenge his foul and most unnatural murder.   25
Hamlet. Murder?
Ghost.
Murder most foul, as in the best it is;°
But this most foul, strange, and unnatural.
Hamlet.
Haste me to know't, that I, with wings as swift
As meditation or the thoughts of love,   30
May sweep to my revenge.
Ghost.   I find thee apt;
And duller shouldst thou be than the fat weed
That rots itself in ease on Lethe wharf,°
Wouldst thou not stir in this. Now, Hamlet, hear:
'Tis given out that, sleeping in my orchard,   35
A serpent stung me; so the whole ear of Denmark
Is by a forged process° of my death
Rankly abused;° but know, thou noble youth,
The serpent that did sting thy father's life
Now wears his crown.
Hamlet.   O my prophetic soul!   40
My uncle?
Ghost.
Ay, that incestuous, that adulterate° beast,

---

20.   **porpentine:** porcupine.
21.   **eternal blazon:** next world.
27.   **as ... is:** as it is [foul] even with the best motives.
32–33. **And ... wharf:** and even if you were more lethargic than the
        thick weed that rots undisturbed at the wharf of the Lethe (the
        river of forgetfulness in Hades).
37.   **forged process:** false account.
38.   **Rankly abused:** utterly deceived.
42.   **adulterate:** adulterous.

With witchcraft of his wit, with traitorous gifts—
O wicked wit and gifts, that have the power
So to seduce!—won to his shameful lust   45
The will of my most seeming-virtuous queen.
O Hamlet, what a falling-off was there,
From me, whose love was of that dignity°
That it went hand in hand even with the vow
I made to her in marriage, and to decline   50
Upon a wretch whose natural gifts were poor
To those of mine!
But virtue, as it never will be moved,
Though lewdness court it in a shape of heaven,°
So lust, though to a radiant angel linked,   55
Will sate itself° in a celestial bed
And prey on garbage.
But, soft! methinks I scent the morning air.
Brief let me be. Sleeping within my orchard,
My custom always of the afternoon,   60
Upon my secure hour° thy uncle stole,
With juice of cursed hebenon° in a vial,
And in the porches° of my ears did pour
The leperous distillment,° whose effect
Holds such an enmity with blood of man   65
That swift as quicksilver it courses through
The natural gates and alleys of the body,
And with a sudden vigor it doth posset°
And curd, like eager° droppings into milk,
The thin and wholesome blood; so did it mine,   70
And a most instant tetter barked about,

---

48. **dignity:** worthiness.
54. **Though ... heaven:** though wooed by lust disguised as an angel.
56. **sate itself:** gorge.
61. **secure hour:** time of relaxation.
62. **hebenon:** a poisonous plant.
63. **porches:** entrance.
64. **leperous distillment:** distillation causing leprosy.
68. **posset:** curdle.
69. **eager:** acidic, sour.

Most lazar-like,° with vile and loathsome crust
All my smooth body.
Thus was I, sleeping, by a brother's hand
Of life, of crown, of queen, at once dispatched;°   75
Cut off even in the blossoms of my sin,
Unhous'led, disappointed, unaneled,°
No reck'ning made, but sent to my account
With all my imperfections on my head.
Hamlet.
O, horrible! O, horrible! most horrible!   80
Ghost.
If thou hast nature° in thee, bear it not.
Let not the royal bed of Denmark be
A couch for luxury° and damned incest.
But, howsoever thou pursuest this act,
Taint not thy mind, nor let thy soul contrive   85
Against thy mother aught. Leave her to heaven,
And to those thorns that in her bosom lodge
To prick and sting her. Fare thee well at once,
The glowworm shows the matin° to be near
And gins° to pale his uneffectual fire.°   90
Adieu, adieu, adieu! Remember me.

Exit.

Hamlet.
O all you host of heaven! O earth! What else?
And shall I couple hell? O, fie! Hold, hold, my heart!
And you, my sinews, grow not instant old,
But bear me stiffly up. Remember thee?   95

71–72. And ... lazar-like: and instantaneously the skin broke out all
        over in scabs, like leprosy.
75. **dispatched:** deprived (by death).
76–77. Cut ... unaneled: killed without having received last rites.
81. **nature:** natural feelings.
83. **luxury:** lust.
89. **matin:** morning.
90. **gins:** begins. **uneffectual fire:** The glowworm's fire is made
        ineffectual by daylight.

Ay, thou poor ghost, while memory holds a seat
In this distracted globe.° Remember thee?
Yea, from the table° of my memory
I'll wipe away all trivial fond° records,
All saws° of books, all forms,° all pressures° past   100
That youth and observation copied there,
And thy commandment all alone shall live
Within the book and volume of my brain,
Unmixed with baser matter. Yes, by heaven!
O most pernicious woman!   105
O villain, villain, smiling, damned villain!
My tables,° my tables! Meet it is° I set it down
That one may smile, and smile, and be a villain;
At least I'm sure it may be so in Denmark.

Writes.

So, uncle, there you are.° Now to my word:°   110
It is "Adieu, adieu! Remember me."
I have sworn't.
Horatio. [*Within.*]
  My lord, my lord!

Enter HORATIO *and* MARCELLUS.

Marcellus.   Lord Hamlet!
Horatio.   Heaven secure° him!
Hamlet. So be it!
Horatio.
  Illo, ho, ho, my lord!   115

---

97.   **globe:** head.
98.   **table:** tablet (notebook).
99.   **fond:** foolish.
100. **saws:** maxims. **forms:** images. **pressures:** impressions.
107. **tables:** See note for line 98. **Meet it is:** It is fitting (that).
110. **there you are:** refers to what he has just "set down." **word:** motto.
      (Hamlet has taken the Ghost's parting words as his motto, or cue
      to action.)
113. **secure:** protect.

Hamlet.
Hillo, ho, ho, boy! Come, bird, come.°
Marcellus.
How is't, my noble lord?
Horatio.   What news, my lord?
Hamlet.
O, wonderful!
Horatio.
Good my lord, tell it.
Hamlet.   No, you'll reveal it.
Horatio.
Not I, my lord, by heaven!
Marcellus.   Nor I, my lord.   120
Hamlet.
How say you, then? Would heart of man once° think it?
But you'll be secret?
Horatio and Marcellus. Ay, by heaven, my lord.
Hamlet.
There's ne'er a villain dwelling in all Denmark
But he's an arrant° knave.
Horatio.
There needs no ghost, my lord, come from the grave   125
To tell us this.
Hamlet.   Why, right! You are i' the right!
And so, without more circumstance° at all,
I hold it fit that we shake hands and part;
You, as your business and desire shall point you,
For every man hath business and desire,   130
Such as it is; and for mine own poor part,
Look you, I'll go pray.
Horatio.
These are but wild and whirling words, my lord.

---

116. **Hillo ... come:** This cry was used by falconers to call back their
      falcons.
121. **once:** ever.
124. **arrant:** downright. (Hamlet stops short of revealing Claudius' crime
      and so turns his sentence into a joking truism.)
127. **circumstance:** ado.

Hamlet.
  I'm sorry they offend you, heartily;
  Yes, faith heartily.
Horatio.   There's no offense, my lord.   135
Hamlet.
  Yes, by Saint Patrick, but there is, Horatio,
  And much offense too. Touching this vision here,
  It is an honest° ghost, that let me tell you.
  For your desire to know what is between us,
  O'ermaster't as you may. And now, good friends,   140
  As you are friends, scholars, and soldiers,
  Give me one poor request.
Horatio.
  What is't, my lord? We will.
Hamlet.
  Never make known what you have seen tonight.
Horatio and Marcellus.
  My lord, we will not.
Hamlet.   Nay, but swear't.
Horatio.   In faith,   145
  My lord, not I.°
Marcellus.   Nor I, my lord, in faith.
Hamlet.
  Upon my sword.°
Marcellus.   We have sworn, my lord, already.
Hamlet.
  Indeed, upon my sword, indeed.

GHOST *cries from beneath the stage.*

Ghost. Swear.
Hamlet.
  Aha boy, say'st thou so? Art thou there, truepenny? °   150

---

138. **honest:** genuine. (That is, the Ghost is not a demon in disguise.)
146. **not I:** I will not make it known. (It does not mean "I will not swear it.")
147. **Upon my sword:** The hilt and blade of a sword form a cross, upon which oaths were often taken.
150. **truepenny:** good fellow.

Come on! You hear this fellow in the cellarage.
Consent to swear.

Horatio.   Propose the oath, my lord.

Hamlet.

Never to speak of this that you have seen.
Swear by my sword.

Ghost. [*Beneath.*] Swear.   155

Hamlet.

Hic et ubique?° Then we'll shift our ground.
Come hither, gentlemen,
And lay your hands again upon my sword.
Never to speak of this that you have heard:
Swear by my sword.   160

Ghost. [*Beneath.*] Swear by his sword.

Hamlet.

Well said, old mole! Canst work i' the earth so fast?
A worthy pioner!° Once more remove,° good friends.

Horatio.

O day and night, but this is wondrous strange!

Hamlet.

And therefore as a stranger give it welcome.°   165
There are more things in heaven and earth, Horatio,
Than are dreamt of in your philosophy.°
But come!
Here, as before, never, so help you mercy,
How strange or odd soe'er I bear myself,   170
As I perchance hereafter shall think meet°
To put an antic disposition° on,
That you, at such times seeing me, never shall,

---

156. **Hic et ubique?:** Latin for "here and everywhere?"
163. **pioner:** miner, digger. **remove:** move.
165. **as ... welcome:** Give it the courteous welcome that is a stranger's
      due.
167. **your philosophy:** not in Horatio's personal beliefs but in philosophy
      in general.
171. **meet:** appropriate.
172. **antic disposition:** insane behavior.

With arms encumb'red thus, or this headshake,°
Or by pronouncing of some doubtful phrase,   175
   As "Well, well, we know," or "We could, an if we
      would,"
Or "If we list° to speak," or "There be, an if they
      might,"°
Or such ambiguous giving out, to note
That you know aught of me—this not to do,
So grace and mercy at your most need help you,°   180
Swear.

Ghost. [*Beneath.*] Swear.

They swear.

Hamlet.
   Rest, rest, perturbed spirit! So, gentlemen,
   With all my love I do commend me to you;
   And what so poor a man as Hamlet is   185
   May do t' express his love and friending° to you,
   God willing, shall not lack. Let us go in together;
   And still° your fingers on your lips, I pray.
   The time is out of joint. O cursed spite°
   That ever I was born to set it right!   190
   Nay, come, let's go together.

                                  Exeunt.

---

174. **With ... headshake:** with arms folded or with your heads nodding
     knowingly.
177. **list:** wished. **"There . . . might":** "There are those who could tell if
     they were allowed to."
180. **So ... you:** so that grace and mercy at your time of greatest need may
     help you.
186. **friending:** friendship.
188. **still:** always.
189. **spite:** affliction.

Act II

Scene 1. *A room in Polonius' house.*

Enter POLONIUS *and* REYNALDO.

Polonius.
　Give him this money and these notes, Reynaldo.
Reynaldo. I will, my lord.
Polonius.
　You shall do marvell's° wisely, good Reynaldo,
　Before you visit him, to make inquire
　Of his behavior.
Reynaldo.　　　　My lord, I did intend it.　　　　　5
Polonius.
　Marry, well said, very well said. Look you, sir,
　Enquire me first what Danskers° are in Paris;
　And how, and who, what means,° and where they
　　keep,°
　What company, at what expense; and finding
　By this encompassment and drift of question°　　10
　That they do know my son, come you more nearer
　Than your particular demands will touch it.°
　Take° you, as 'twere, some distant knowledge of him;
　As thus, "I know his father and his friends,
　And in part him." Do you mark this, Reynaldo?　　15
Reynaldo. Ay, very well, my lord.
Polonius.
　"And in part him, but" you may say, "not well.
　But, if 't be he I mean, he's very wild,

II.1.3. **marvell's:** marvelously.
7.　　**Danskers:** Danes.
8.　　**what means:** what their income is. **keep:** lodge.
10.　**encompassment ... question:** roundabout inquiry.
11–12. **come ... it:** You will find out more than you would by asking direct
　　　 questions.
13.　**Take:** assume.

Addicted so and so"; and there put on him°
What forgeries° you please; marry, none so rank°   20
As may dishonor him—take heed of that;
But, sir, such wanton,° wild, and usual slips
As are companions noted and most known
To youth and liberty.
Reynaldo.   As gaming,° my lord.
Polonius.
Ay, or drinking, fencing, swearing, quarreling,   25
Drabbing.° You may go so far.
Reynaldo.
My lord, that would dishonor him.
Polonius.
Faith, no, as you may season it in the charge.°
You must not put another scandal on him,
That he is open to incontinency.°   30
That's not my meaning. But breathe his faults so
      quaintly°
That they may seem the taints of liberty,°
The flash and outbreak of a fiery mind,
A savageness in unreclaimed° blood,
Of general assault.°
Reynaldo.   But, my good lord—   35
Polonius.
Wherefore should you do this?
Reynaldo.   Ay, my lord,
I would know that.

---

19.   **put on him:** charge him with.
20.   **forgeries:** fabrications. **rank:** great.
22.   **wanton:** unrestrained.
24.   **gaming:** gambling.
26.   **Drabbing:** consorting with loose women.
28.   **season … charge:** soften the seriousness of the charge.
30.   **incontinency:** debauchery.
31.   **quaintly:** cleverly.
32.   **taints of liberty:** faults resulting from having unlimited freedom.
34.   **unreclaimed:** untamed.
35.   **Of … assault:** common to all people.

Polonius.   Marry, sir, here's my drift,°
And I believe it is a fetch of warrant.°
You laying these slight sullies on my son
As 'twere a thing a little soiled i' the working,°   40
Mark you,
Your party in converse,° him you would sound,
Having ever seen in the prenominate° crimes
The youth you breathe of guilty, be assured
He closes with you in this consequence:°   45
"Good sir," or so, or "friend," or "gentleman"—
According to the phrase or the addition°
Of man and country—
Reynaldo.   Very good, my lord.
Polonius.
And then, sir, does he this—he does—
What was I about to say? By the mass, I was   50
about to say something! Where did I leave?
Reynaldo.
At "closes in the consequence," at "friend or
so," and "gentleman."
Polonius.
At "closes in the consequence"—Ay, marry!
He closes thus: "I know the gentleman.   55
I saw him yesterday, or t'other day,
Or then, or then, with such or such; and, as you say,
There was he gaming; there o'ertook in 's rouse;°
There falling out at tennis"; or perchance,
"I saw him enter such a house of sale,"   60
Videlicet,° a brothel, or so forth.

---

37.   **drift:** scheme.
38.   **fetch of warrant:** legitimate trick.
40.   **As ... working:** as an article becomes soiled in the process of making it (so will a young man in the process of growing up).
42.   **converse:** conversation.
43.   **prenominate:** previously named.
45.   **closes ... consequence:** agrees with you in what follows as a result.
47.   **addition:** title added to a person's name.
58.   **o'ertook ... rouse:** overcome by drink (drunk).
61.   **Videlicet:** Latin for "namely."

See you now—
Your bait of falsehood takes this carp° of truth;
And thus do we of wisdom and of reach,°
With windlasses and with assays of bias,°   65
By indirections find directions out.
So by my former lecture and advice,
Shall you my son. You have me,° have you not?

Reynaldo.
My lord, I have.

Polonius.   God be wi' you, fare you well!

Reynaldo. Good my lord!   70

Polonius.
Observe his inclination in yourself.°

Reynaldo. I shall, my lord.

Polonius.
And let him ply his music.°

Reynaldo.   Well, my lord.

Polonius.
Farewell!

                                        Exit REYNALDO.

Enter OPHELIA.

              How now, Ophelia? What's the matter?

Ophelia.
O, my lord, my lord, I have been so affrighted!   75

Polonius.
With what, i' the name of God?

Ophelia.
My lord, as I was sewing in my closet,°

---

63. **carp:** kind of fish.
64. **And ... reach:** And this is what we people of wisdom and under-
     standing do.
65. **With ... bias:** with roundabout courses and devious approaches.
68. **have me:** understand me.
71. **in yourself:** with your own eyes.
73. **ply his music:** do as he pleases. (That is, don't interfere; just observe.)
77. **closet:** private room.

Lord Hamlet, with his doublet all unbraced,°
No hat upon his head, his stockings fouled,
Ungart'red, and down-gyved° to his ankle;   80
Pale as his shirt, his knees knocking each other,
And with a look so piteous in purport°
As if he had been loosed out of hell
To speak of horrors—he comes before me.
Polonius.
    Mad for thy love?
Ophelia.   My lord, I do not know,   85
    But truly, I do fear it.
Polonius.   What said he?
Ophelia.
    He took me by the wrist and held me hard;
    Then goes he to the length of all his arm,°
    And, with his other hand thus o'er his brow,
    He falls to such perusal of my face   90
    As he would draw it.° Long stayed he so.
    At last, a little shaking of mine arm,
    And thrice his head thus waving up and down,
    He raised a sigh so piteous and profound
    As it did seem to shatter all his bulk°   95
    And end his being. That done, he lets me go,
    And with his head over his shoulder turned
    He seemed to find his way without his eyes,
    For out o' doors he went without their help
    And to the last bended their light on me.   100
Polonius.
    Come, go with me. I will go seek the King.
    This is the very ecstasy° of love,

---

78.   **doublet all unbraced:** jacket unfastened.
80.   **down-gyved:** hanging down in coils.
82.   **purport:** meaning.
88.   **goes … arm:** moves back until he is holding me at arm's length.
91.   **As … it:** as if he intended to sketch it.
95.   **bulk:** torso.
102. **ecstasy:** madness.

Whose violent property° fordoes° itself
And leads the will to desperate undertakings
As oft as any passion under heaven   105
That does afflict our natures. I am sorry.
What, have you given him any hard words of late?
Ophelia.
No, my good lord; but, as you did command,
I did repel his letters and denied
His access to me.
Polonius.   That hath made him mad.   110
I am sorry that with better heed and judgment
I had not quoted° him. I feared he did but trifle
And meant to wrack° thee; but beshrew my jealousy!°
By heaven, it is as proper to our age
To cast beyond ourselves in our opinions   115
As it is common for the younger sort
To lack discretion. Come, go we to the King.
This must be known; which, being kept close, might
    move
More grief to hide than hate to utter love.°
Come.   120

                                                    Exeunt.

Scene 2. *A room in the castle.*

Flourish. Enter KING CLAUDIUS, QUEEN GERTRUDE, ROSEN-
CRANTZ, GUILDENSTERN, *and* ATTENDANTS.

---

103. **property:** characteristic. **fordoes:** destroys. (Those driven to madness
      by love are in danger of committing suicide.)
112. **quoted:** observed.
113. **wrack:** ruin. **beshrew my jealousy:** curse my mistrust.
118–119. **which ... love:** which, if not mentioned, might cause more grief
      (because Hamlet might be suicidal) than it would cause offense if it
      were made known.

King.

Welcome, dear Rosencrantz and Guildenstern.
Moreover° that we much did long to see you,
The need we have to use you did provoke°
Our hasty sending. Something have you heard
Of Hamlet's transformation. So call it,   5
Sith nor° the exterior nor the inward man
Resembles that it was. What it should be,
More than his father's death, that thus hath put him
So much from the understanding of himself,
I cannot dream of. I entreat you both   10
That, being of so young days brought up with him,°
And since so neighbored to his youth and havior,
That you vouchsafe your rest° here in our court
Some little time; so by your companies
To draw him on to pleasures, and to gather   15
So much as from occasion° you may glean,
Whether aught to us unknown afflicts him thus
That, opened,° lies within our remedy.

Queen.

Good gentlemen, he hath much talked of you,
And sure I am two men there are not living   20
To whom he more adheres.° If it will please you
To show us so much gentry° and good will
As to expend your time with us awhile
For the supply and profit of our hope,°
Your visitation shall receive such thanks   25
As fits a king's remembrance.

II.2.2. **Moreover:** besides.
3.   **provoke:** cause.
6.   **Sith nor:** since neither.
11.   **being ... him:** because you grew up together.
13.   **vouchsafe your rest:** consent to stay.
16.   **occasion:** opportunity.
18.   **opened:** revealed.
21.   **To ... adheres:** whom he regards more highly.
22.   **gentry:** courtesy.
24.   **For ... hope:** for the purpose of fulfilling our hopes.

Rosencrantz.   Both your Majesties
  Might, by the sovereign power you have of us,
  Put your dread° pleasures more into command
  Than to entreaty.
Guildenstern.   But we both obey,
  And here give up ourselves, in the full bent°   30
  To lay our service freely at your feet,
  To be commanded.
King.
  Thanks, Rosencrantz and gentle Guildenstern.
Queen.
  Thanks, Guildenstern and gentle Rosencrantz.
  And I beseech you instantly to visit   35
  My too much changed son. —Go, some° of you,
  And bring these gentlemen where Hamlet is.
Guildenstern.
  Heavens make our presence and our practices°
  Pleasant and helpful to him!
Queen.   Ay, amen!

Exeunt ROSENCRANTZ, GUILDENSTERN, *and some* ATTENDANTS.
Enter POLONIUS.

Polonius.
  The ambassadors from Norway, my good lord,   40
  Are joyfully returned.
King.
  Thou still hast been° the father of good news.
Polonius.
  Have I, my lord? I assure my good liege,
  I hold my duty as I hold my soul,
  Both to my God and to my gracious king;   45

---

28. **dread:** respected.
30. **in ... bent:** to the utmost. (The image is that of a bow fully bent to
     release an arrow as far as possible.)
36. **some:** one.
38. **practices:** doings (and, ironically, deceits).
42. **Thou ... been:** you have always been.

And I do think—or else this brain of mine
Hunts not the trail of policy so sure°
As it hath used to do—that I have found
The very cause of Hamlet's lunacy.

King. •

O, speak of that! That do I long to hear.   50

Polonius.

Give first admittance to the ambassadors,
My news shall be the fruit° to that great feast.

King.

Thyself do grace to them,° and bring them in.

Exit POLONIUS.

He tells me, my dear Gertrude, he hath found
The head and source of all your son's distemper.°   55

Queen.

I doubt° it is no other but the main,°
His father's death and our o'erhasty marriage.

King.

Well, we shall sift° him.

Enter POLONIUS *with* VOLTEMAND *and* CORNELIUS.

Welcome, my good friends.
Say, Voltemand, what from our brother Norway?

Voltemand.

Most fair return of greetings and desires.°   60
Upon our first,° he sent out to suppress
His nephew's levies,° which to him appeared
To be a preparation 'gainst the Polack,

---

47.   **Hunts ... sure:** does not follow the trail of political intrigue as surely.
52.   **fruit:** dessert.
53.   **do ... them:** honor them (by escorting them).
55.   **distemper:** emotional upset.
56.   **doubt:** suspect. **main:** main cause.
58.   **sift:** question closely.
60.   **desires:** good wishes.
61.   **Upon our first:** as a result of our first audience.
62.   **levies:** raising of armies.

But, better looked into, he truly found
It was against your Highness; whereat grieved,   65
That so his sickness, age, and impotence
Was falsely borne in hand,° sends out arrests
On Fortinbras;° which he, in brief, obeys,
Receives rebuke from Norway, and, in fine,°
Makes vow before his uncle never more   70
To give the assay of arms° against your Majesty.
Whereon old Norway, overcome with joy,
Gives him three thousand crowns in annual fee
And his commission to employ those soldiers,
So levied as before, against the Polack;   75
With an entreaty, herein further shown,

Gives a paper.

That it might please you to give quiet pass°
Through your dominions for this enterprise,
On such regards of safety and allowance
As therein are set down.
King.   It likes us well;°   80
And at our more considered time° we'll read,
Answer, and think upon this business.
Meantime we thank you for your well-took labor.
Go to your rest; at night we'll feast together.
Most welcome home!

                    Exeunt VOLTEMAND *and* CORNELIUS.

Polonius.   This business is well ended.   85
My liege, and madam, to expostulate°

---

67.   **borne in hand:** interpreted.
67–68. **arrests ... Fortinbras:** orders for Fortinbras to stop.
69.   **in fine:** in the end.
71.   **assay of arms:** test of strength.
77.   **quiet pass:** peaceful passage. (Shakespeare mistakenly believes
       that Denmark lies between Norway and Poland.)
80.   **likes us well:** pleases me.
81.   **at ... time:** when we have time to consider it at greater length.
86.   **expostulate:** inquire into.

What majesty should be, what duty is,
Why day is day, night night, and time is time,°
Were nothing but to waste night, day, and time.
Therefore, since brevity is the soul of wit,   90
And tediousness the limbs and outward flourishes,°
I will be brief. Your noble son is mad.
Mad call I it; for, to define true madness,
What is't but to be nothing else but mad?
But let that go.
Queen. More matter, with less art.°   95
Polonius.
Madam, I swear I use no art at all.
That he is mad, 'tis true: 'tis true 'tis pity;
And pity 'tis 'tis true. A foolish figure!°
But farewell it, for I will use no art.
Mad let us grant him then. And now remains   100
That we find out the cause of this effect—
Or rather say, the cause of this defect,
For this effect defective comes by cause.°
Thus it remains, and the remainder thus.
Perpend:°   105
I have a daughter (have while she is mine),
Who in her duty and obedience, mark,
Hath given me this. Now gather, and surmise. °

[*Reads.*]

    To the celestial and my soul's idol, the most beautified°
      Ophelia—

87–88. **what duty … time:** The essential meaning of this is "Explaining a
    subject's duty is as unnecessary as explaining day and night."
91.   **flourishes:** nonessential decoration.
95.   **art:** eloquence.
98.   **figure:** figure of speech.
103. **comes by cause:** must have a cause.
105. **Perpend:** Consider.
108. **surmise:** draw your own conclusions.
109. **beautified:** beautiful.

That's an ill phrase, a vile phrase; "beautified" is a
    vile phrase.   110
But you shall hear. Thus:

[*Reads.*]

In her excellent white bosom, these, &c.
Queen. Came this from Hamlet to her?
Polonius. Good madam, stay awhile. I will be faithful.

[*Reads.*]

          Doubt thou the stars are fire;   115
          Doubt that the sun doth move;
            Doubt truth to be a liar;
            But never doubt I love.
O dear Ophelia, I am ill at these numbers;° I
have not art to reckon my groans;° but that I love   120
thee best, O most best, believe it. Adieu.
          Thine evermore most dear lady,
          whilst this machine is to him,°

                           HAMLET.

This, in obedience, hath my daughter shown me;
And more above, hath his solicitings,   125
As they fell out by time, by means, and place,
All given to mine ear.°
King.   But how hath she
Received his love?
Polonius.   What do you think of me?
King.
As of a man faithful and honorable.
Polonius.
I would fain° prove so. But what might you think,   130

---

119. **ill ... numbers:** untalented at writing verses.
120. **reckon my groans:** summarize my sighs as a lover.
123. **whilst ... him:** while I still inhabit this body.
125–27. **And ... ear:** And in addition, she has reported all his attentions to
      her as they occurred.
130. **fain:** willingly.

When I had seen this hot love on the wing
(As I perceived it, I must tell you that,
Before my daughter told me), what might you,
Or my dear Majesty your queen here, think,
If I had played the desk or table book,°   135
Or given my heart a winking,° mute and dumb,
Or looked upon this love with idle sight?
What might you think? No, I went round° to work
And my young mistress thus I did bespeak:
"Lord Hamlet is a prince, out of thy star.°   140
This must not be." And then I precepts gave her,
That she should lock herself from his resort,°
Admit no messengers, receive no tokens.
Which done, she took the fruits of my advice,°
And he, repulsed, a short tale to make,   145
Fell into a sadness, then into a fast,
Thence to a watch, thence into a weakness,
Thence to a lightness, and, by this declension,
Into the madness wherein now he raves,°
And all we mourn for.

King.   Do you think 'tis this?   150

Queen.

It may be, very like.

Polonius.

Hath there been such a time—I would fain know that—
That I have positively said "'Tis so,"
When it proved otherwise?

King.   Not that I know.

---

135. **played ... book:** acted as a go-between.
136. **given ... winking:** did not concern myself.
138. **round:** straight.
140. **out ... star:** with a higher status.
142. **resort:** access.
144. **took ... advice:** obeyed.
146–49. **Fell into ... raves:** Polonius describes the symptoms of what he
       considers to be a classic case: first melancholy; then loss of appetite,
       sleeplessness, physical weakness, and mental aberrations; and
       finally insanity.

Polonius. [*Points to his head and shoulder.*]
    Take this from this, if this be otherwise.   155
    If circumstances lead me, I will find
    Where truth is hid, though it were hid indeed
    Within the center.°
King.   How may we try it further?
Polonius.
    You know sometimes he walks four hours together°
    Here in the lobby.
Queen.   So he does indeed.   160
Polonius. At such a time I'll loose° my daughter
    to him.
    Be you and I behind an arras° then.
    Mark the encounter. If he love her not,
    And be not from his reason fall'n thereon,°
    Let me be no assistant for a state,   165
    But keep a farm and carters.
King.   We will try it.

Enter HAMLET, *reading a book.*

Queen.
    But look where sadly the poor wretch comes reading.
Polonius.
    Away, I do beseech you, both away!
    I'll board him presently.° O, give me leave.

Exeunt KING CLAUDIUS, QUEEN GERTRUDE, *and* ATTENDANTS.

    How does my good Lord Hamlet?   170
Hamlet. Well, God-a-mercy.
Polonius. Do you know me, my lord?
Hamlet. Excellent well. You are a fishmonger.°

---

158. **center:** center of the earth.
159. **four ... together:** several hours in all.
161. **loose:** turn loose.
162. **arras:** tapestry hung on walls.
164. **thereon:** on that account.
169. **board him presently:** accost him immediately.
173. **fishmonger:** a seller of fish; its slang meaning was "pimp."

Polonius. Not I, my lord.

Hamlet. Then I would you were so honest a man. 175

Polonius. Honest, my lord?

Hamlet. Ay, sir. To be honest, as this world goes, is to
be one man picked out of ten thousand.

Polonius. That's very true, my lord.

Hamlet. For if the sun breed maggots in a dead dog,° 180
being a god° kissing carrion—Have you a daughter?

Polonius. I have, my lord.

Hamlet. Let her not walk i' the sun. Conception° is a
blessing, but not as your daughter may conceive.
Friend, look to't. 185

Polonius. [*Aside.*] How say you by that? Still
harping on my daughter. Yet he knew me not at
first. He said I was a fishmonger. He is far gone,
far gone! And truly in my youth I suff'red much
extremity for love—very near this. I'll speak to 190
him again. —What do you read, my lord?

Hamlet. Words, words, words.

Polonius. What is the matter,° my lord?

Hamlet. Between who?

Polonius. I mean, the matter that you read, 195
my lord.

Hamlet. Slanders, sir; for the satirical rogue says here
that old men have gray beards; that their faces
are wrinkled; their eyes purging° thick amber and
plum-tree gum; and that they have a plentiful lack 200
of wit, together with most weak hams.° All which,
sir, though I most powerfully and potently believe,

---

180. **the sun ... dog:** a general belief at that time.
181. **god:** In some editions this word is *good*; the expression would then
mean "carrion that is good to kiss."
183. **Conception:** The word can mean both "the formation of ideas" and
"becoming pregnant."
193. **matter:** Hamlet purposely misunderstands *matter* (meaning
"subject matter") as "quarrel."
199. **purging:** discharging.
201. **hams:** thigh area behind the knees.

yet I hold it not honesty° to have it thus set down;
for yourself, sir, should be old as I am if, like a crab,
you could go backward.   205

Polonius. [*Aside.*] Though this be madness, yet
there is method° in't. —Will you walk out of the air,
my lord?

Hamlet. Into my grave?

Polonius. Indeed, that is out o' the air.   210
[*Aside.*] How pregnant° sometimes his replies are!
a happiness° that often madness hits on, which
reason and sanity could not so prosperously be
delivered of. I will leave him, and suddenly°
contrive the means of meeting between him and   215
my daughter. —My honorable lord, I will most
humbly take my leave of you.

Hamlet. You cannot, sir, take from me anything that I
will more willingly part withal—except my life,
except my life, except my life.   220

Enter ROSENCRANTZ *and* GUILDENSTERN.

Polonius. Fare you well, my lord.

Hamlet. These tedious old fools!

Polonius. You go to seek the Lord Hamlet. There
he is.

Rosencrantz. [*To* POLONIUS.] God save you, sir!   225

                                            Exit POLONIUS.

Guildenstern. My honored lord!

Rosencrantz. My most dear lord!

---

203. **honesty:** proper conduct.
207. **method:** sense, reason.
211. **pregnant:** quick-witted.
212. **happiness:** fortunate choice of words.
214. **suddenly:** immediately.

Hamlet. My excellent good friends! How dost thou, Guildenstern! Ah, Rosencrantz! Good lads, how do ye both? 230

Rosencrantz.
As the indifferent° children of the earth.

Guildenstern.
Happy in that we are not over-happy.
On Fortune's cap we are not the very button.°

Hamlet. Nor the soles of her shoe?

Rosencrantz. Neither, my lord. 235

Hamlet. Then you live about her waist, or in the middle of her favors?

Guildenstern. Faith, her privates° we.

Hamlet. In the secret parts of Fortune? O, most true! she is a strumpet.° What news? 240

Rosencrantz. None, my lord, but that the world's grown honest.

Hamlet. Then is doomsday near! But your news is not true. Let me question more in particular. What have you, my good friends, deserved at the hands 245 of Fortune that she sends you to prison° hither?

Guildenstern. Prison, my lord?

Hamlet. Denmark's a prison.

Rosencrantz. Then is the world one.

Hamlet. A goodly° one; in which there are many 250 confines, wards,° and dungeons, Denmark being one o' the worst.

Rosencrantz. We think not so, my lord.

---

231. **indifferent:** doing neither well nor badly.
233. **button:** the topmost part of a cap.
238. **privates:** The word means both "private parts of the body" and "citizens without rank."
240. **strumpet:** Hamlet calls Fortune a strumpet because of her fickle nature.
246. **prison:** The feeling of being in prison was thought to be a symptom of melancholy.
250. **goodly:** good-sized.
251. **wards:** prison cells.

Hamlet. Why, then 'tis none to you, for there is nothing
either good or bad but thinking makes it so. /   255.
To me it is a prison.

Rosencrantz. Why, then your ambition makes it one.
'Tis too narrow for your mind.

Hamlet. O God, I could be bounded in a nutshell
and count myself a king of infinite space, were it   260
not that I have bad dreams.

Guildenstern. Which dreams indeed are ambition; for
the very substance of the ambitious is merely the
shadow of a dream.

Hamlet. A dream itself is but a shadow.   265

Rosencrantz. Truly, and I hold ambition of
so airy and light a quality that it is but a shadow's
shadow.

Hamlet. Then are our beggars bodies, and our
monarchs and outstretched heroes the beggars'   270
shadows.° Shall we to the court? for, by my fay,°
I cannot reason.°

Rosencrantz and Guildenstern. We'll wait upon you.

Hamlet. No such matter! I will not sort you with
the rest of my servants;° for, to speak to you like an   275
honest man, I am most dreadfully attended.° But,
in the beaten way° of friendship, what make you at
Elsinore?

Rosencrantz. To visit you, my lord; no other occasion.

Hamlet. Beggar that I am, I am even poor in thanks;   .   280
but I thank you; and sure, dear friends, my thanks
are too dear a halfpenny.° Were you not sent for?

269–71. Then ... shadows: If ambition is a "shadow's shadow," then beggars, who lack ambition, are solid flesh. Monarchs and heroes, who are ambitious, are shadows.

271. fay: faith.

272. reason: argue.

274–75. I ... servants: Hamlet purposely misunderstands *wait upon* to mean "serve" instead of "accompany."

276. dreadfully attended: The term can mean both "poorly served" and "attended by dread."

277. beaten way: well-worn path.

282. too ... halfpenny: not worth a halfpenny.

Is it your own inclining? Is it a free visitation?°
Come, deal justly° with me. Come, come! Nay,
speak.   285
Guildenstern. What should we say, my lord?
Hamlet. Why, anything, but to the purpose.° You were
sent for, and there is a kind of confession in your
looks, which your modesties have not craft enough
to color.° I know the good King and Queen have   290
sent for you.
Rosencrantz. To what end, my lord?
Hamlet. That you must teach me. But let me conjure°
you by the rights of our fellowship, by the consonancy
of our youth,° by the obligation of our ever-preserved 295
love, and by what more dear° a better proposer
could charge you withal, be even° and direct with
me, whether you were sent for, or no.
Rosencrantz. [*Aside to* GUILDENSTERN.] What say you?
Hamlet. [*Aside.*] Nay then, I have an eye of° you.   300
If you love me, hold not off.°
Guildenstern. My lord, we were sent for.
Hamlet. I will tell you why, so shall my anticipation
prevent your discovery, and your secrecy to the
King and Queen molt no feather.° I have of late—   305
but wherefore I know not—lost all my mirth,
forgone all custom of exercises; and indeed, it goes
so heavily with my disposition that this goodly
frame, the earth, seems to me a sterile promontory;

---

283. **free visitation:** voluntary visit.
284. **justly:** honestly.
287. **but ... purpose:** except the truth.
290. **color:** disguise.
293. **conjure:** beg; ask earnestly.
294–95. **consonancy ... youth:** harmony we had as youngsters.
296. **dear:** important (things).
297. **even:** straightforward.
300. **of:** on.
301. **hold not off:** do not hang back.
303–05. **so ... feather:** so my discussing it in advance will come before you
reveal it, and your pledge of secrecy to the king and queen will not
then be violated.

this most excellent canopy, the air, look you, this   310
brave o'erhanging firmament,° this majestical roof
fretted with golden fire°—why, it appeareth no other
thing to me than a foul and pestilent congregation
of vapors. What a piece of work is a man! how noble
in reason! how infinite in faculty!° in form and   315
moving how express° and admirable! in action how
like an angel! in apprehension how like a god! the
beauty of the world, the paragon of animals! And
yet to me what is this quintessence° of dust? Man
delights not me—no, nor woman neither, though   320
by your smiling you seem to say so.
Rosencrantz. My lord, there was no such stuff in my
thoughts.
Hamlet. Why did you laugh then, when I said
"Man delights not me"?   325
Rosencrantz. To think, my lord, if you delight not in
man, what lenten entertainment° the players
shall receive from you. We coted° them on the way,
and hither are they coming to offer you service.
Hamlet. He that plays the king shall be welcome—his   330
Majesty shall have tribute of me; the adventurous
knight shall use his foil and target;° the lover shall
not sigh gratis;° the humorous° man shall end
his part in peace; the clown shall make those laugh
whose lungs are tickled o' the sere;° and the lady   335
shall say her mind freely, or the blank verse° shall
halt° for't. What players are they?

---

311. **brave … firmament:** splendid sky overhead.
312. **fretted … fire:** star-studded.
315. **faculty:** ability.
316. **express:** precise.
319. **quintessence:** concentrated essence.
327. **lenten entertainment:** meager reception.
328. **coted:** passed.
332. **foil and target:** sword and shield.
333. **gratis:** free. **humorous:** governed by moods or whims.
335. **tickled … sere:** easily triggered to laughter.
336. **blank verse:** unrhymed iambic pentameter.
337. **halt:** proceed lamely.

Rosencrantz. Even those you were wont to° take such
delight in, the tragedians of the city.

Hamlet. How chances it they travel? Their residence, 340
both in reputation and profit, was better both ways.°

Rosencrantz. I think their inhibition° comes by the
means of the late innovation.

Hamlet. Do they hold the same estimation° they did
when I was in the city? Are they so followed? 345

Rosencrantz. No, indeed, are they not.

Hamlet. How comes it? Do they grow rusty?

Rosencrantz. Nay, their endeavor keeps in the wonted
pace; but there is, sir, an eyrie° of children, little
eyases,° that cry out on the top of question and are 350
most tyrannically clapped for't. These are now the
fashion, and so berattle the common stages (so they
call them) that many wearing rapiers are afraid
of goosequills° and dare scarce come thither.

Hamlet. What, are they children? Who maintains 'em? 355
How are they escoted?° Will they pursue the
quality° no longer than they can sing?° Will they
not say afterwards, if they should grow themselves
to common players (as it is most like, if their means
are no better), their writers do them wrong to make 360
them exclaim against their own succession?

Rosencrantz. Faith, there has been much to do on
both sides; and the nation holds it no sin to tarre°

---

338. **were wont to:** used to.
340–41. **Their ... ways:** If they stayed in the city, they would gain in fame
and profit.
342. **inhibition:** ban (against playing in the city).
344. **Do ... estimation:** Are they still held in esteem?
349. **eyrie:** nest.
350. **eyases:** noisy young hawks. Shakespeare is referring to the groups of
boy actors.
353–54. **many ... goosequills:** many brave men fear public criticism.
(Goosequills are pens.)
356. **escoted:** supported.
357. **quality:** profession. **no ... sing:** only until their voices change.
363. **tarre:** incite.

them to controversy. There was, for a while, no
money bid for argument unless the poet and the   365
player went to cuffs in the question.°
Hamlet. Is't possible?
Guildenstern. O, there has been much throwing about
of brains.
Hamlet. Do the boys carry it away?°   370
Rosencrantz. Ay, that they do, my lord—Hercules
and his load° too.
Hamlet. It is not very strange; for my uncle is King of
Denmark, and those that would make mows° at
him while my father lived give twenty, forty, fifty,   375
a hundred ducats apiece for his picture in little.°
'Sblood, there is something in this more than
natural, if philosophy could find it out.

Flourish for the PLAYERS.

Guildenstern. There are the players.
Hamlet. Gentlemen, you are welcome to Elsinore.   380
Your hands, come! The appurtenance° of welcome
is fashion and ceremony. Let me comply with you
in this garb,° lest my extent° to the players (which
I tell you must show fairly outwards) should more
appear like entertainment than yours. You are   385
welcome. But my uncle-father and aunt-mother
are deceived.
Guildenstern. In what, my dear lord?

364–66. There … question: No producer wanted a play without a quarrel
between a poet from one camp and a player from another.
370. carry it away: win.
371–72. Hercules … load: the world, which in Greek mythology Atlas held
on his shoulders and Hercules relieved him of for a while.
374. mows: faces.
376. picture in little: miniature.
381. appurtenance: pertinent part.
382–83. comply … garb: observe the formalities with you in this fashion
(by shaking hands with the players).
383. extent: behavior.

Hamlet. I am but mad north-north-west. When the
    wind is southerly I know a hawk from a handsaw.°   390

Enter POLONIUS.

Polonius. Well be with you, gentlemen!
Hamlet. Hark you, Guildenstern—and you too—at
    each ear a hearer! That great baby you see there
    is not yet out of his swaddling clouts.°
Rosencrantz. Happily he's the second time come to   395
    them; for they say an old man is twice a child.
Hamlet. I will prophesy he comes to tell me of the
    players. Mark it. —You say right, sir; a Monday
    morning; 'twas so indeed.°
Polonius. My lord, I have news to tell you.   400
Hamlet. My lord, I have news to tell you: when
    Roscius° was an actor in Rome—
Polonius. The actors are come hither, my lord.
Hamlet. Buzz, buzz!
Polonius. Upon mine honor—   405
Hamlet. Then came each actor on his ass°—
Polonius. The best actors in the world, either
    for tragedy, comedy, history, pastoral, pastoral-
    comical, historical-pastoral, tragical-historical,
    tragical-comical-historical-pastoral; scene   410
    individable, or poem unlimited. Seneca° cannot be

389–90. I ... handsaw: People believed that southerly winds were best for
    melancholy. Hamlet is saying that when his mental state is at its best,
    he can tell one thing from another, and knows what's what.
394. clouts: clothes.
398–99. You ... indeed: Hamlet is ignoring Polonius by pretending to be
    talking seriously to Rosencrantz.
402. Roscius (c. 126–62 B.C.): a famous actor in ancient Rome. Hamlet
    implies that Polonius brings stale news.
406. Then ... ass: line from a song. Again, Hamlet mocks Polonius'
    last words.
411. Seneca (c. 4 B.C.–A.D. 65): Roman writer of tragedies.

too heavy, nor Plautus° too light. For the law of
writ and the liberty,° these are the only men.
Hamlet. O Jephthah,° judge of Israel, what a
    treasure hadst thou!   415
Polonius. What a treasure had he, my lord?
Hamlet. Why,
> One fair daughter and no more,
> The which he loved passing° well.
Polonius. [*Aside.*] Still on my daughter.   420
Hamlet. Am I not i' the right, old Jephthah?
Polonius. If you call me Jephthah, my lord, I
    have a daughter that I love passing well.
Hamlet. Nay, that follows not.°
Polonius. What follows then, my lord?   425
Hamlet. Why,
> As by lot, God wot,°
and then, you know,
> It came to pass, as most like it was.
The first row° of the pious chanson° will show   430
you more; for look where my abridgment° comes.

Enter four or five PLAYERS.

You are welcome, masters; welcome, all. —I am glad
to see thee well. —Welcome, good friends. —O, my
old friend? Why, thy face is valanced° since I saw
thee last. Comest thou to beard° me in Denmark?—   435

---

412. **Plautus (c. 254–184 B.C.):** Roman writer of comic plays.
412–13. **For ... liberty:** For writing that observes both rules and freedom.
414. **Jephthah:** a Biblical judge who sacrificed his daughter.
419. **passing:** exceedingly.
424. **that ... not:** Hamlet means that just because Polonius has a daughter,
    he doesn't necessarily love her as Jephthah loved his daughter.
427. **wot:** knows.
430. **row:** stanza. **pious chanson:** song with a Biblical subject.
431. **abridgment:** The word can mean both "interruption" and "enter-
    tainment."
434. **valanced:** bearded.
435. **beard:** confront (a play on words).

What, my young lady° and mistress! By'r Lady, your
ladyship is nearer to heaven than when I saw you
last by the altitude of a chopine.° Pray God, your
voice, like a piece of uncurrent gold, be not cracked
within the ring.°—Masters, you are all welcome.   440
We'll e'en to't like French falconers, fly at anything we
see. We'll have a speech straight. Come, give us a
taste of your quality. Come, a passionate speech.

First Player. What speech, my lord?

Hamlet. I heard thee speak me a speech once, but it   445
was never acted; or, if it was, not above once; for
the play, I remember, pleased not the million, 'twas
caviary to the general;° but it was (as I received it,
and others, whose judgments in such matters cried
in the top of mine) an excellent play, well digested   450
in the scenes, set down with as much modesty
as cunning. I remember, one said there were no
sallets° in the lines to make the matter savory, nor
no matter in the phrase that might indict the author of
affectation; but called it an honest method, as   455
wholesome as sweet, and by very much more
handsome than fine. One speech in it I chiefly loved.
'Twas Aeneas'° tale to Dido,° and thereabout of it
especially where he speaks of Priam's° slaughter.
If it live in your memory, begin at this line—let me   460
see, let me see:

---

436. **young lady:** boy actor who played women's roles.
438. **chopine:** a woman's thick-soled shoe. (The boy actor has grown
     taller.)
438–40. **Pray ... ring:** If the boy's voice changes, he can't play female roles.
     The comparison is to a gold coin that has had its edges clipped, mak-
     ing it valueless.
448. **caviary ... general:** wasted on the general public.
453. **sallets:** a variant of *salads*, meaning "spicy morsels, ribaldry."
458. **Aeneas:** the hero of the *Aeneid*, an epic by the Roman poet Virgil
     (70–19 B.C.). **Dido:** in the *Aeneid*, a queen of Carthage, loved by
     Aeneas.
459. **Priam:** in Greek and Roman mythology, the king of Troy.

  The rugged Pyrrhus° like the Hyrcanian beast°—
'Tis not so; it begins with Pyrrhus:
  The rugged Pyrrhus, he whose sable arms,°
  Black as his purpose, did the night resemble   465
  When he lay couched in the ominous horse,°
  Hath now this dread and black complexion° smeared
  With heraldry more dismal. Head to foot
  Now is he total gules,° horridly tricked°
  With blood of fathers, mothers, daughters, sons, 470
  Baked and impasted with the parching streets,
  That lend a tyrannous° and a damned light
  To their lord's murder. Roasted in wrath and fire,
  And thus o'ersized° with coagulate gore,
  With eyes like carbuncles,° the hellish Pyrrhus 475
  Old grandsire Priam seeks.
 So, proceed you.
Polonius. Fore God, my lord, well spoken, with
 good accent and good discretion.
First Player.   *Anon he finds him* 480
  Striking too short at Greeks. His antique° sword,
  Rebellious to his arm, lies where it falls,
  Repugnant to command.° Unequal matched,
  Pyrrhus at Priam drives, in rage strikes wide;
  But with the whiff and wind of his fell° sword 485
  The unnerved father falls. Then senseless° Ilium,°

---

462. **Pyrrhus:** in Greek and Roman mythology, son of Achilles, who
  avenged his father's death by killing Priam. **Hyrcanian beast:** tiger.
464. **sable arms:** black armor.
466. **ominous horse:** in legend, hollow wooden horse from which the
  Greeks emerged to destroy Troy.
467. **complexion:** figure.
469. **gules:** red. **tricked:** outlined.
472. **tyrannous:** harsh.
474. **o'ersized:** smeared over.
475. **like carbuncles:** with a reddish glow.
481. **antique:** long used.
483. **Repugnant to command:** refusing to be used.
485. **fell:** cruel.
486. **senseless:** having no feeling. **Ilium:** Troy's citadel.

Seeming to feel this blow, with flaming top
Stoops° to his base, and with a hideous crash
Takes prisoner Pyrrhus' ear. For, lo! his sword,
Which was declining° on the milky° head   490
Of reverend Priam, seemed i' the air to stick.
So, as a painted° tyrant, Pyrrhus stood,
And like a neutral to his will and matter,°
Did nothing.
But, as we often see,° against° some storm,   495
A silence in the heavens, the rack° stand still,
The bold winds speechless, and the orb below
As hush as death—anon the dreadful thunder
Doth rend the region; so, after Pyrrhus' pause,
Aroused vengeance sets him new awork;   500
And never did the Cyclops' hammers° fall
On Mars's° armor, forged for proof eterne,°
With less remorse than Pyrrhus' bleeding sword
Now falls on Priam.
Out, out, thou strumpet Fortune! All you gods,   505
In general synod take away her power;
Break all the spokes and fellies from her wheel,
And bowl the round nave down the hill of heaven,
As low as to the fiends!

Polonius. This is too long.   510

Hamlet. It shall to the barber's, with your beard.

—Prithee say on. He's for a jig° or a tale of

---

488.   **Stoops:** collapses.
490.   **declining:** descending. **milky:** milk-white.
492.   **painted:** motionless (as if in a painting).
493.   **like … matter:** immobilized between desire and action.
495.   **see:** perceive. **against:** as a preliminary to.
496.   **rack:** high clouds.
501.   **Cyclops' hammers:** In Greek mythology, the Cyclopes were giants who worked for Vulcan, the smith and armor maker of the gods.
502.   **Mars:** Roman god of war. **forged … eterne:** strong enough to last eternally.
512.   **jig:** short farce, including dancing and singing.

bawdry, or he sleeps. Say on; come to Hecuba.°
First Player.
 But who, ah woe! had seen the mobled° queen—
Hamlet. "The mobled queen"?   515
Polonius. That's good! "Mobled queen" is good.
First Player.
 Run barefoot up and down, threat'ning the flames
 With bisson rheum;° a clout° upon that head
 Where late the diadem° stood, and for a robe,
 About her lank and all o'erteemed° loins,   520
 A blanket, in the alarm of fear caught up—
 Who this had seen, with tongue in venom steeped
 'Gainst Fortune's state would·treason have pronounced.°
 But if the gods themselves did see her then,
 When she saw Pyrrhus make malicious sport   525
 In mincing with his sword her husband's limbs,
 The instant burst of clamor that she made
 (Unless things mortal move them not at all)
 Would have made milch the burning eyes of heaven°
 And passion in the gods.   530
Polonius. Look, wh'er° he has not turned his
 color and has tears in's° eyes. Prithee no more!
Hamlet. 'Tis well. I'll have thee speak out the rest
 soon.—Good my lord, will you see the players
 well bestowed?° Do you hear? Let them be well 535
 used; for they are the abstract and brief chronicles
 of the time.° After your death you were better

---

513. **Hecuba:** in mythology, queen of Troy.
514. **mobled:** muffled.
518. **bisson rheum:** blinding tears. **clout:** cloth.
519. **diadem:** crown.
520. **o'erteemed:** exhausted from childbearing.
523. **'Gainst ... pronounced:** would have denounced Fortune's control of people's lives.
529. **Would ... heaven:** would have elicited the milk of tears from the stars.
531. **wh'er:** whether.
532. **in's:** in his.
535. **bestowed:** lodged.
536–37. **the abstract ... time:** short, up-to-date news items.

have a bad epitaph than their ill report while you
live.

Polonius. My lord, I will use them according to 540
their desert.

Hamlet. God's bodykins,° man, much better! Use
every man after his desert,° and who should scape
whipping? Use them after your own honor and
dignity. The less they deserve, the more merit is in 545
your bounty. Take them in.

Polonius. Come, sirs.

Hamlet. Follow him, friends. We'll hear a play
tomorrow.

> *Exit* POLONIUS *with all the* PLAYERS *but the* FIRST.

Dost thou hear me, old friend; can you play "The 550
Murder of Gonzago"?

First Player. Ay, my lord.

Hamlet. We'll ha't° tomorrow night. You could,
for a need,° study a speech of some dozen or sixteen
lines which I would set down and insert in't, could 555
you not?

First Player. Ay, my lord.

Hamlet. Very well. Follow that lord—and look
you mock him not.

> *Exit* FIRST PLAYER.

My good friends, I'll leave you till night. You 560
are welcome to Elsinore.

Rosencrantz. Good my lord!

Hamlet.
Ay, so, God be wi' ye!

> *Exeunt* ROSENCRANTZ *and* GUILDENSTERN.

---

542. **bodykins:** dear body.
543. **after his desert:** according to what he deserves.
553. **ha't:** have it.
554. **for a need:** if you need to.

Now I am alone.
O, what a rogue and peasant° slave am I!
Is it not monstrous that this player here,   565
But in a fiction, in a dream of passion,°
Could force his soul so to his own conceit°
That, from her working,° all his visage wanned,°
Tears in his eyes, distraction in's aspect,°
A broken voice, and his whole function suiting   570
With forms to his conceit? And all for nothing!
For Hecuba!
What's Hecuba to him, or he to Hecuba,
That he should weep for her? What would he do,
Had he the motive and the cue for passion   575
That I have? He would drown the stage with tears
And cleave the general ear° with horrid speech;
Make mad the guilty and appal the free,°
Confound the ignorant, and amaze indeed
The very faculties of eyes and ears.   580
Yet I,
A dull and muddy-mettled° rascal, peak°
Like John-a-dreams, unpregnant of my cause,°
And can say nothing! No, not for a king,
Upon whose property° and most dear life   585
A damned defeat was made. Am I a coward?
Who calls me villain? breaks my pate° across?
Plucks off my beard and blows it in my face?
Tweaks me by the nose? gives me the lie° i' the throat
As deep as to the lungs? Who does me this, ha?   590

---

564. **peasant:** low.
566. **dream of passion:** pretended emotion.
567. **to ... conceit:** into alignment with what he has created in his mind.
568. **from her working:** as a result of the soul's creativity. **wanned:** paled.
569. **distraction in's aspect:** frenzy in his appearance.
577. **general ear:** the audience.
578. **Make ... free:** drive the guilty insane and frighten the innocent.
582. **muddy-mettled:** dull in spirit. **peak:** mope.
583. **Like ... cause:** like a dreamy fellow, not taking action to further my
        cause.
585. **property:** life.
587. **pate:** head.
589. **gives ... lie:** calls me a liar.

'Swounds, I should take it! for it cannot be
But I am pigeon-livered and lack gall
To make oppression bitter, or ere this
I should have fatted all the region kites°
With this slave's offal.° Bloody, bawdy villain!   595
Remorseless,° treacherous, lecherous, kindless°
  villain!
O, vengeance!
Why, what an ass am I! This is most brave,°
That I, the son of a dear father murdered,   600
Prompted to my revenge by heaven and hell,
Must (like a whore) unpack° my heart with words
And fall a-cursing like a very drab,°
A scullion! °
Fie upon't! foh! About,° my brain! I have heard   605
That guilty creatures, sitting at a play,
Have by the very cunning° of the scene
Been struck so to the soul that presently°
They have proclaimed their malefactions;°
For murder, though it have no tongue, will speak   610
With most miraculous organ. I'll have these players
Play something like the murder of my father
Before mine uncle. I'll observe his looks,
I'll tent° him to the quick; if he but blench,°
I know my course. The spirit that I have seen   615

---

594. **region kites:** birds of prey of the air.
595. **offal:** entrails.
596. **remorseless:** pitiless. **kindless:** unnatural.
599. **brave:** admirable.
602. **unpack:** unburden.
603. **drab:** slut.
604. **scullion:** menial kitchen worker.
605. **About:** Get going.
607. **cunning:** art.
608. **presently:** immediately.
609. **proclaimed their malefactions:** confessed their evil deeds.
614. **tent:** probe. **blench:** flinch.

May be the devil; and the devil hath power
T' assume a pleasing shape; yea, and perhaps
Out of my weakness and my melancholy,
As he is very potent with such spirits,
Abuses° me to damn me. I'll have grounds   620
More relative° than this. The play's the thing
Wherein I'll catch the conscience of the King.

Exit.

---

620.   Abuses: deceives.
621.   relative: compelling.

Act III

Scene 1. *A room in the castle.*

Enter KING CLAUDIUS, QUEEN GERTRUDE, POLONIUS, OPHELIA,
ROSENCRANTZ, *and* GUILDENSTERN.

King.
 And can you, by no drift of circumstance,°
 Get from him why he puts on this confusion,
 Grating so harshly all his days of quiet
 With turbulent and dangerous lunacy?
Rosencrantz.
 He does confess he feels himself distracted,°   5
 But from what cause he will by no means speak.
Guildenstern.
 Nor do we find him forward to be sounded,°
 But with a crafty madness keeps aloof
 When we would bring him on to some confession
 Of his true state.
Queen.   Did he receive you well?   10
Rosencrantz.
 Most like a gentleman.
Guildenstern.
 But with much forcing of his disposition.°
Rosencrantz.
 Niggard of question, but of our demands
 Most free in his reply.°
Queen.   Did you assay him
 To any pastime?   15
Rosencrantz.
 Madam, it so fell out that certain players

III.1.1. **circumstance:** conversation.
5. **distracted:** mentally confused.
7. **forward ... sounded:** open to questioning.
12. **disposition:** inclination.
13–14. **Niggard ... reply:** conversing very little but straightforward in
   answering our questions.

We o'erraught° on the way. Of these we told him,
And there did seem in him a kind of joy
To hear of it. They are about the court,
And, as I think, they have already order   20
This night to play before him.

Polonius.   'Tis most true;
And he beseeched me to entreat your Majesties
To hear and see the matter.

King.
With all my heart, and it doth much content me
To hear him so inclined.   25
Good gentlemen, give him a further edge°
And drive his purpose on to these delights.

Rosencrantz.
We shall, my lord.

Exeunt ROSENCRANTZ *and* GUILDENSTERN.

King.   Sweet Gertrude, leave us too;
For we have closely sent for Hamlet hither,
That he, as 'twere by accident, may here   30
Affront Ophelia.°
Her father and myself (lawful espials)°
Will so bestow ourselves that, seeing unseen,
We may of their encounter frankly judge
And gather by him, as he is behaved,°   35
If't be the affliction of his love, or no,
That thus he suffers for.

Queen.   I shall obey you;
And for your part, Ophelia, I do wish
That your good beauties be the happy cause
Of Hamlet's wildness. So shall I hope your virtues   40

---

17. **o'erraught:** overtook.
26. **edge:** inducement.
31. **Affront Ophelia:** meet Ophelia face-to-face.
32. **espials:** spies.
35. **by ... behaved:** from the way he behaves.

Will bring him to his wonted way° again,
To both your honors.

Ophelia. Madam, I wish it may.

Exit QUEEN GERTRUDE.

Polonius.
Ophelia, walk you here. —Gracious,° so please you,
We will bestow ourselves. [*To* OPHELIA.] Read
  on this book,
That show of such an exercise may color   45
Your loneliness.° —We are oft to blame in this,
'Tis too much proved,° that with devotion's visage°
And pious action we do sugar o'er
The devil himself.

King. [*Aside.*] O, 'tis too true!
How smart a lash that speech doth give my
  conscience   50
The harlot's cheek, beautied with plast'ring art,
Is not more ugly to° the thing that helps it
Than is my deed to my most painted word.
O heavy burden!

Polonius.
I hear him coming. Let's withdraw, my lord.   55

Exeunt KING CLAUDIUS and POLONIUS.

Enter HAMLET.

Hamlet.
To be,° or not to be, that is the question:
Whether 'tis nobler in the mind to suffer

---

41. **wonted way:** normal condition.
43. **Gracious:** Your Majesty (said to the king).
45–46. **That … loneliness:** so that your reading might be an excuse for
        your being alone.
47. **proved:** shown by experience. **devotion's visage:** outward show of
        religious fervor.
52. **to:** compared to.
56. **To be:** To go on living.

The slings and arrows of outrageous° fortune
Or to take arms against a sea of troubles,
And by opposing end them. To die—to sleep—   60
No more; and by a sleep to say we end
The heartache, and the thousand natural shocks
That flesh is heir to. 'Tis a consummation°
Devoutly to be wished. To die—to sleep.
To sleep—perchance to dream: ay, there's the rub!°   65
For in that sleep of death what dreams may come
When we have shuffled off this mortal coil,°
Must give us pause. There's the respect
That makes calamity of so long life.°
For who would bear the whips and scorns of time,   70
The oppressor's wrong, the proud man's contumely,
The pangs of despised love, the law's delay,
The insolence of office, and the spurns
That patient merit of the unworthy takes,°
When he himself might his quietus° make   75
With a bare bodkin?° Who would fardels° bear,
To grunt and sweat under a weary life,
But that the dread of something after death—
The undiscovered country, from whose bourn
No traveler returns—puzzles the will,   80
And makes us rather bear those ills we have
Than fly to others that we know not of?
Thus conscience does make cowards of us all,
And thus the native hue° of resolution

---

58.   **outrageous:** cruel.
63.   **consummation:** ending.
65.   **rub:** obstacle.
67.   **coil:** turmoil (but also life's entanglements).
68–69. **the respect ... life:** the reason that makes living so long a calamity;
       also, the reason that makes calamity so long-lived.
73–74. **the spurns ... takes:** the insults from the unworthy that people of
       merit must endure patiently.
75.   **quietus:** release.
76.   **bare bodkin:** mere dagger (less likely meaning is "unsheathed
       dagger"). **fardels:** burdens.
84.   **native hue:** reddish complexion.

Is sicklied o'er with the pale cast° of thought,   85
And enterprises of great pith and moment
With this regard their currents turn awry
And lose the name of action.° —Soft you now!
The fair Ophelia! —Nymph, in thy orisons°
Be all my sins rememb'red.

Ophelia.   Good my lord,   90
How does your honor for this many a day?

Hamlet.
I humbly thank you; well, well, well.

Ophelia.
My lord, I have remembrances of yours,
That I have longed long° to redeliver;
I pray you, now receive them.

Hamlet.   No, not I!   95
I never gave you aught.

Ophelia.
My honored lord, you know right well you did,
And with them words of so sweet breath composed
As made the things more rich. Their perfume lost,
Take these again; for to the noble mind   100
Rich gifts wax poor when givers prove unkind.
There, my lord.

Hamlet. Ha, ha! Are you honest?°

Ophelia. My lord?

Hamlet. Are you fair?   105

Ophelia. What means your lordship?

Hamlet. That if you be honest and fair, your honesty
should admit no discourse° to your beauty.

---

85.   **cast:** color.
87–88. **With … action:** Brooding on this thought causes great enterprises to
    be diverted from their course and left undone.
89.   **orisons:** prayers.
94.   **longed long:** wished for a long time. (*Longed* is pronounced as two
    syllables.)
103.   **honest:** sincere, chaste.
108.   **discourse:** approach.

Ophelia. Could beauty, my lord, have better
    commerce than with honesty?   110

Hamlet. Ay, truly; for the power of beauty will
    sooner transform honesty from what it is to a bawd°
    than the force of honesty can translate beauty into
    his° likeness. This was sometime a paradox,° but
    now the time gives it proof. I did love you once.   115

Ophelia. Indeed, my lord, you made me believe so.

Hamlet. You should not have believed me; for
    virtue cannot so inoculate our old stock but we
    shall relish of it.° I loved you not.

Ophelia. I was the more deceived.   120

Hamlet. Get thee to a nunnery! Why wouldst thou
    be a breeder of sinners? I am myself indifferent
    honest,° but yet I could accuse me of such things
    that it were better my mother had not borne me.
    I am very proud, revengeful, ambitious; with   125
    more offenses at my beck° than I have thoughts to
    put them in, imagination to give them shape, or
    time to act them in. What should such fellows as
    I do, crawling between earth and heaven? We are
    arrant° knaves all; believe none of us. Go thy   130
    ways to a nunnery. Where's your father?

Ophelia. At home, my lord.

Hamlet. Let the doors be shut upon him, that he
    may play the fool nowhere but in's own house.
    Farewell.   135

Ophelia. O, help him, you sweet heavens!

---

112.   **bawd:** procurer.
114.   **his:** its. **sometime a paradox:** formerly a belief contrary to public
     opinion.
118–19.   **virtue ... it:** Grafting virtue onto ourselves cannot completely
     eliminate the trace of sinfulness in us.
122–23. **indifferent honest:** moderately virtuous.
126.   **at my beck:** available to me.
130.   **arrant:** out-and-out.

Hamlet. If thou dost marry, I'll give thee this
plague for thy dowry: be thou as chaste as ice,
as pure as snow, thou shalt not escape calumny.
Get thee to a nunnery. Go, farewell. Or if thou   140
wilt needs marry, marry a fool; for wise men
know well enough what monsters° you make of
them. To a nunnery, go; and quickly too. Farewell.
Ophelia. O heavenly powers, restore him!
Hamlet. I have heard of your paintings too, well   145
enough. God has given you one face, and you
make yourselves another. You jig, you amble, and
you lisp;° you nickname° God's creatures and
make your wantonness your ignorance.° Go to, I'll
no more on't!° it hath made me mad. I say, we   150
will have no mo marriages. Those that are
married already—all but one—shall live; the
rest shall keep as they are. To a nunnery, go.

                                                  Exit.

Ophelia.
O, what a noble mind is here o'erthrown!
The courtier's, soldier's, scholar's, eye, tongue,
     sword,   155
The expectancy and rose of the fair state,°
The glass° of fashion and the mold of form,°
The observed° of all observers—quite, quite down!

---

142. **monsters:** cuckolds (deceived husbands). (Cuckolds were depicted
     with horns.)
147–48. **jig ... lisp:** dance, strut, talk affectedly.
148. **nickname:** find new names for.
149. **make ... ignorance:** what you do as an affectation you pretend you
     do because of ignorance.
150. **on't:** of it.
156. **The expectancy ... state:** the country's heir to the throne and ideal
     person.
157. **glass:** mirror. **mold of form:** model of behavior.
158. **observed:** respected.

And I, of ladies most deject and wretched,
That sucked the honey of his music vows,   160
Now see that noble and most sovereign reason,
Like sweet bells jangled, out of tune and harsh;
That unmatched form and feature of blown° youth
Blasted with ecstasy.° O, woe is me
T' have seen what I have seen, see what I see!   165

Enter KING CLAUDIUS *and* POLONIUS.

King.

Love? his affections° do not that way tend;
Nor what he spake, though it lacked form a little,
Was not like madness. There's something in his soul
O'er which his melancholy sits on brood;°
And I do doubt° the hatch and the disclose°   170
Will be some danger; which for to prevent,
I have in quick determination
Thus set it down:° he shall with speed to England
For the demand of our neglected tribute.°
Haply° the seas and countries different,   175
With variable objects,° shall expel
This something°-settled matter in his heart,
Whereon his brains still beating puts him thus
From fashion of himself.° What think you on't?

---

163. **blown:** full-blown.
164. **Blasted with ecstasy:** ruined by madness.
166. **affections:** inclinations, feelings.
169. **on brood:** hatching.
170. **doubt:** fear. **disclose:** what will be revealed (at the hatching).
173. **set it down:** decided.
174. **tribute:** payment.
175. **Haply:** perhaps.
176. **variable objects:** various sights.
177. **something:** sometimes defined as "somewhat"; more likely it means
      "undefined."
179. **fashion of himself:** normal behavior.

Polonius.

It shall do well. But yet do I believe   180
The origin and commencement of his grief
Sprung from neglected love. —How now, Ophelia?
You need not tell us what Lord Hamlet said,
We heard it all. —My lord, do as you please;
But, if you hold it fit, after the play   185
Let his queen mother all alone entreat him
To show his grief. Let her be round° with him;
And I'll be placed, so please you, in the ear
Of all their conference. If she find him not,°
To England send him; or confine him where   190
Your wisdom best shall think.

King.   It shall be so.
Madness in great ones must not unwatched go.

                                 Exeunt.

Scene 2. *A hall in the castle.*

Enter HAMLET *and three of the* PLAYERS.

Hamlet. Speak the speech,° I pray you, as I
pronounced it to you, trippingly on the tongue.
But if you mouth it,° as many of your players do,
I had as lief° the town crier spoke my lines. Nor do
not saw the air too much with your hand, thus, but   5
use all gently; for in the very torrent, tempest, and
(as I may say) whirlwind of passion, you must
acquire and beget a temperance that may give it

---

187.   **round:** blunt.
189.   **find him not:** does not find out the source of his problem.
III.2.1. the speech: the speech Hamlet wrote for the players.
3.   **mouth it:** ham it up.
4.   **had as lief:** would just as soon.

smoothness. O, it offends me to the soul to hear a
robustious° periwig-pated fellow tear a passion to   10
tatters, to very rags, to split the ears of the
groundlings,° who (for the most part) are capable
of nothing but inexplicable dumb shows and noise,°
I would have such a fellow whipped for o'erdoing
Termagant.° It out-herods Herod.° Pray you   15
avoid it.

First Player. I warrant your honor.

Hamlet. Be not too tame neither; but let your own
discretion be your tutor. Suit the action to the
word, the word to the action; with this special   20
observance, that you o'erstep not the modesty° of
nature: for anything so overdone is from the purpose
of playing, whose end, both at the first and now,
was and is, to hold, as 'twere, the mirror up to
nature; to show virtue her own feature, scorn her   25
own image, and the very age and body of the time
his form and pressure.° Now this overdone, or
come tardy off, though it make the unskillful°
laugh, cannot but make the judicious grieve; the
censure of the which one° must in your allowance   30
o'erweigh a whole theater of others. O, there
be players that I have seen play, and heard
others praise, and that highly (not to speak it
profanely), that, neither having the accent of
Christians, nor the gait of Christian, pagan,   35

---

10. **robustious:** ranting.
12. **groundlings:** spectators who paid the least and had to stand in the yard.
12–13. **are ... noise:** appreciate spectacle and mere noise more than sense.
15. **Termagant:** in medieval drama, a noisy character. **Herod:** a Biblical tyrant, depicted in medieval drama as violent and raging.
21. **modesty:** moderation.
26–27. **very ... pressure:** an exact impression of the age.
28. **unskillful:** undiscriminating.
30. **censure ... one:** opinion of the judicious spectator.

nor man,° have so strutted and bellowed that I
have thought some of Nature's journeymen° had
made men, and not made them well, they imitated
humanity so abominably.

First Player. I hope we have reformed that   40
indifferently° with us, sir.

Hamlet. O, reform it altogether! And let those that
play your clowns speak no more than is set
down for them. For there be of them that will
themselves laugh, to set on some quantity   45
of barren spectators to laugh too, though in the
meantime some necessary question of the play be
then to be considered. That's villainous and shows
a most pitiful ambition in the fool that uses it.
Go make you ready.   50

Exeunt PLAYERS.

Enter POLONIUS, ROSENCRANTZ, *and* GUILDENSTERN.

How now, my lord? I will the King hear this
piece of work?°

Polonius. And the Queen too, and that presently.°

Hamlet. Bid the players make haste.

Exit POLONIUS.

Will you two help to hasten them?   55

Rosencrantz and Guildenstern. We will, my lord.

Exeunt ROSENCRANTZ *and* GUILDENSTERN.

Hamlet. What ho, Horatio!

Enter HORATIO.

Horatio. Here, sweet lord, at your service.

---

36. **nor man:** nor of anyone whatever.
37. **journeymen:** hired workers.
41. **indifferently:** pretty well.
52. **piece of work:** composition.
53. **presently:** right away.

Hamlet.
>Horatio, thou art e'en as just° a man
>As e'er my conversation coped withal.°   60
Horatio.
>O, my dear lord!
Hamlet.   Nay, do not think I flatter;
>For what advancement may I hope from thee,
>That no revenue° hast but thy good spirits
>To feed and clothe thee? Why should the poor
>   be flattered?
>No, let the candied tongue lick absurd pomp,   65
>And crook the pregnant hinges of the knee
>Where thrift may follow fawning.° Dost thou hear?
>Since my dear soul was mistress of her choice
>And could of men distinguish, her election
>Hath sealed thee for herself. For thou hast been   70
>As one, in suff'ring all, that suffers nothing;
>A man that Fortune's buffets and rewards
>Hast ta'en with equal thanks; and blest are those
>Whose blood° and judgment are so well commingled
>That they are not a pipe° for Fortune's finger   75
>To sound what stop° she please. Give me that man
>That is not passion's slave, and I will wear him
>In my heart's core, ay, in my heart of heart,
>As I do thee. Something too much of this!
>There is a play tonight before the King.   80
>One scene of it comes near the circumstance,
>Which I have told thee, of my father's death.

---

59.   **just:** well-balanced.
60.   **As ... withal:** as I ever encountered in my dealings with people.
63.   **revenue:** The stress is often put on the second syllable.
65–67. **let ... fawning:** let flatterers speak sugar-coated words to insipid ("absurd") pomp and be always ready ("pregnant") to kneel if profit ("thrift") can result.
74.   **blood:** passion.
75.   **pipe:** wind instrument.
76.   **sound what stop:** play whatever note.

I prithee, when thou seest that act afoot,
Even with the very comment° of thy soul
Observe my uncle. If his occulted° guilt   85
Do not itself unkennel in one speech,°
It is a damned ghost that we have seen,
And my imaginations are as foul
As Vulcan's stithy.° Give him heedful note;
For I mine eyes will rivet to his face,   90
And after we will both our judgments join
In censure of his seeming.°
Horatio.   Well, my lord.
If he steal aught the whilst this play is playing,
And scape detecting, I will pay the theft.
Hamlet. They are coming to the play: I must be idle.°   95
Get you a place.

Sound a flourish. Enter trumpets and kettledrums. Danish march.
Enter KING CLAUDIUS, QUEEN GERTRUDE, POLONIUS, OPHELIA,
ROSENCRANTZ, GUILDENSTERN, *and other* LORDS.

King. How fares° our cousin Hamlet?
Hamlet. Excellent, i' faith, of the chameleon's dish:°
I eat the air, promise-crammed. You cannot feed
capons so.   100
King. I have nothing with this answer, Hamlet.
These words are not mine.°

---

84.   **very comment:** close observation.
85.   **occulted:** hidden.
86.   **one speech:** the speech written by Hamlet.
89.   **Vulcan's stithy:** the anvil of Vulcan, the smith of the Roman gods.
92.   **In ... seeming:** in forming an opinion about his outward appearance.
95.   **be idle:** seem insane.
97.   **fares:** is (but Hamlet chooses its other meaning, "eats").
98.   **chameleon's dish:** The chameleon was thought to be able to live on a
      diet of air.
101–02. **I ... mine:** I don't understand your answer, Hamlet. It doesn't
      relate to my question.

Hamlet. No, nor mine now.° [*To* POLONIUS.] My lord,
you played once i' the university, you say?

Polonius. That did I, my lord, and was   105
accounted a good actor.

Hamlet. What did you enact?

Polonius. I did enact Julius Caesar; I was killed
i' the Capitol; Brutus killed me.

Hamlet. It was a brute part of him to kill so capital   110
a calf there. Be the players ready?

Rosencrantz. Ay, my lord. They stay upon your
patience.°

Queen. Come hither, my dear Hamlet, sit
by me.   115

Hamlet. No, good mother, here's metal more
attractive.°

Polonius. [*To the* KING.] O, ho! do you
mark that?

Hamlet. Lady, shall I lie in your lap?   120

Lies at OPHELIA's *feet.*

Ophelia. No, my lord.

Hamlet. I mean, my head upon your lap?

Ophelia. Ay, my lord.

Hamlet. Do you think I meant country matters?°

Ophelia. I think nothing, my lord.   125

Hamlet. That's a fair thought to lie between maids'
legs.

Ophelia. What is, my lord?

Hamlet. Nothing.

Ophelia. You are merry, my lord.   130

Hamlet. Who, I?

Ophelia. Ay, my lord.

---

103. **nor mine now:** Words, once spoken, no longer belong to the speaker.
112–13. **stay ... patience:** wait until you are ready to hear them.
116–17. **metal ... attractive:** a double meaning of "metal with attractive
    properties" and "nicer person."
124. **country matters:** lewd behavior.

Hamlet. O God, your only jig-maker!° What should
   a man do but be merry? For look you how
   cheerfully my mother looks, and my father died   135
   within 's two hours.
Ophelia. Nay, 'tis twice two months, my lord.
Hamlet. So long? Nay then, let the devil wear
   black, for I'll have a suit of sables.° O heavens!
   die two months ago, and not forgotten yet? Then   140
   there's hope a great man's memory may outlive
   his life half a year. But, by'r Lady, he must build
   churches, then; or else shall he suffer not thinking
   on,° with the hobby-horse,° whose epitaph is
   "For O, for O, the hobby-horse is forgot!"   145

Hautboys play. The dumb show enters.

Enter a KING *and a* QUEEN *very lovingly; the* QUEEN
*embracing him, and he her. She kneels, and makes show of
protestation unto him. He takes her up, and declines his head
upon her neck. He lays him down upon a bank of flowers.
She, seeing him asleep, leaves him. Anon comes in a fellow,
takes off his crown, kisses it, and pours poison in the* KING's
ears, and exits. The QUEEN *returns; finds the* KING *dead, and
makes passionate action. The* POISONER, *with some two or
three* MUTES, *comes in again, seeming to lament with her. The
dead body is carried away. The* POISONER *woos the* QUEEN
*with gifts; she seems loath and unwilling awhile, but in the
end accepts his love.*

                                                    Exeunt.

Ophelia. What means this, my lord?
Hamlet. Marry, this is miching mallecho;° it
   means mischief.

---

133. **jig-maker:** composer of jigs, champion entertainer.
139. **sables:** *sable* meant "black" as well as "a kind of fur."
143–44. **suffer … on:** endure not being remembered.
144. **hobby-horse:** figure of a horse associated with morris dances and
     the May games and banned by the Puritans.
147. **miching mallecho:** underhanded evildoing.

Ophelia. Belike° this show imports the argument°
of the play.   150

Enter PLAYER *as* PROLOGUE.

Hamlet. We shall know by this fellow.° The players
cannot keep counsel; they'll tell all.
Ophelia. Will he tell us what this show meant?
Hamlet. Ay, or any show that you'll show him. Be
not you ashamed to show, he'll not shame to tell   155
you what it means.
Ophelia. You are naught, you are naught!° I'll
mark° the play.
Prologue.
For us, and for our tragedy,
Here stooping to your clemency,   160
We beg your hearing patiently.

Exit.

Hamlet. Is this a prologue, or the posy° of a ring?
Ophelia. 'Tis brief, my lord.
Hamlet. As woman's love.

Enter two PLAYERS *as* KING *and* QUEEN.

Player King.
Full thirty times hath Phoebus' cart° gone round   165
Neptune's salt wash° and Tellus' orbed ground,°
And thirty dozen moons with borrowed sheen
About the world have times twelve thirties been,

---

149. **Belike:** perhaps. **imports the argument:** carries the main meaning.
151. **this fellow:** The dumb show traditionally had a presenter, who
       explained the meaning of the pantomime.
157. **naught:** naughty.
158. **mark:** pay attention to.
162. **posy:** short motto.
165. **Phoebus' cart:** the chariot of the sun god.
166. **Neptune's salt wash:** the sea. **Tellus' orbed ground:** the earth.

Since love our hearts, and Hymen° did our hands,
Unite commutual in most sacred bands.°   170

Player Queen.
So many journeys may the sun and moon
Make us again count o'er ere love be done!
But, woe is me! you are so sick of late,
So far from cheer and from your former state,
That I distrust you. Yet, though I distrust,°   175
Discomfort you, my lord, it nothing must;
For women's fear and love holds quantity,°
In neither aught, or in extremity.°
Now, what my love is, proof hath made you know;
And as my love is sized, my fear is so.   180
Where love is great, the littlest doubts are fear;
Where little fears grow great, great love grows there.

Player King.
Faith, I must leave thee,° love, and shortly too;
My operant powers their functions leave to do.°
And thou shalt live in this fair world behind,   185
Honored, beloved, and haply one as kind
For husband shalt thou—

Player Queen.   *O, confound the rest!*
Such love must needs be treason in my breast.
In second husband let me be accurst!
None wed the second but° who killed the first.   190

Hamlet. [*Aside.*] Wormwood, wormwood.°

---

169. **Hymen:** the Greek goddess of marriage.
170. **bands:** bonds.
175. **distrust:** fear for.
177. **holds quantity:** are equal in amount.
178. **in extremity:** feeling either nothing or else too much.
183. **leave thee:** die.
184. **My … do:** my faculties stop working.
190. **but:** except those.
191. **Wormwood:** bitterness.

Player Queen.
> The instances° that second marriage move
> Are base respects of thrift,° but none of love.
> A second time I kill my husband dead
> When second husband kisses me in bed.   195

Player King.
> I do believe you think what now you speak;
> But what we do determine oft we break.
> Purpose is but the slave to memory,
> Of violent birth, but poor validity;°
> Which now, like fruit unripe, sticks on the tree,   200
> But fall unshaken when they mellow be.
> Most necessary 'tis that we forget
> To pay ourselves what to ourselves is debt.°
> What to ourselves in passion we propose,
> The passion ending, doth the purpose lose.   205
> The violence of either grief or joy
> Their own enactures with themselves destroy.°
> Where joy most revels, grief doth most lament;
> Grief joys, joy grieves, on slender accident.°
> This world is not for aye,° nor 'tis not strange   210
> That even our loves should with our fortunes change;
> For 'tis a question left us yet to prove,
> Whether love lead fortune, or else fortune love.
> The great man down, you mark his favorite flies,°
> The poor advanced° makes friends of enemies;   215
> And hitherto doth love on fortune tend,
> For who not needs shall never lack a friend,

---

192. **instances:** motives.
193. **respects of thrift:** consideration of financial gain.
199. **validity:** strength.
202–03. **we … debt:** What we owe ourselves (our resolutions) often remains an unpaid debt.
207. **Their … destroy:** destroys one's ability to take action.
209. **on slender accident:** over trivialities.
210. **aye:** ever.
214. **mark … flies:** notice that his best friend abandons him.
215. **The poor advanced:** the poor person who has become rich.

> And who in want a hollow° friend doth try,
> Directly seasons him° his enemy.
> But, orderly to end where I begun,   220
> Our wills and fates do so contrary run
> That our devices° still are overthrown;
> Our thoughts are ours, their ends° none of our own.
> So think thou wilt no second husband wed;
> But die thy thoughts when thy first lord is dead.   225

Player Queen.
> Nor earth to me give food, nor heaven light,
> Sport and repose lock from me day and night,°
> To desperation turn my trust and hope,
> An anchor's cheer° in prison be my scope,
> Each opposite that blanks the face of joy   230
> Meet what I would have well, and it destroy,°
> Both here and hence° pursue me lasting strife,
> If, once a widow, ever I be wife!

Hamlet. If she should break it now!

Player King.
> 'Tis deeply sworn. Sweet, leave me here awhile.   235
> My spirits grow dull, and fain I would beguile
> The tedious day with sleep.

Player Queen.   Sleep rock thy brain,

[PLAYER KING *sleeps.*]

> And never come mischance between us twain!

>   *Exit.*

Hamlet. Madam, how like you this play?

---

218. **hollow:** insincere.
219. **seasons him:** ripens him into.
222. **devices:** plans.
223. **ends:** results.
227. **Sport … night:** May day deny me pastimes and night deny me sleep (an inverted sentence).
229. **An anchor's cheer:** a hermit's way of life.
230–31. **Each … destroy:** May everything that I hope would succeed meet opposition that would destroy it, turning joy's face pale.
232. **here and hence:** in this world and the next.

Queen. The lady doth protest too much,   240
   methinks.

Hamlet. O, but she'll keep her word.

King. Have you heard the argument?° Is
   there no offense in't?

Hamlet. No, no, they do but jest, poison in jest; no   245
   offense i' the world.

King. What do you call the play?

Hamlet. "The Mousetrap." Marry, how? Tropically.°
   This play is the image of a murder done in Vienna.
   Gonzago is the duke's name: his wife, Baptista.   250
   You shall see anon. 'Tis a knavish piece of work;
   but what o' that? Your Majesty, and we that have
   free souls,° it touches us not. Let the galled jade°
   wince; our withers° are unwrung.

Enter PLAYER *as* LUCIANUS.

   This is one Lucianus, nephew to the King.   255

Ophelia. You are as good as a chorus,° my lord.

Hamlet. I could interpret between you and your love,
   if I could see the puppets dallying.°

Ophelia. You are keen, my lord, you are keen.

Hamlet. It would cost you a groaning to take off my   260
   edge.

Ophelia. Still better, and worse.

Hamlet. So you must take your husbands.° —Begin,
   murderer. Pox, leave thy damnable faces, and

---

243. **argument:** summary of the plot.
248. **Tropically:** metaphorically. (The play is designed to trap the King. *Tropically* is a pun on *trap*.)
253. **free souls:** the innocent. **galled jade:** chafed horse.
254. **withers:** horse's back. (The sentence means "Let the guilty feel the pain; the innocent are untouched by it.")
256. **chorus:** the actors who explain the action of a play.
257–58. **I ... dallying:** Like a puppeteer, I could provide dialogue if I observed you and a lover.
263. **husbands:** Husbands are taken "for better or for worse" according to the marriage vows.

begin! Come, the croaking raven doth bellow for   265
revenge.

Lucianus.
   Thoughts black, hands apt, drugs fit, and time agreeing;
   Confederate season, else no creature seeing;°
   Thou mixture rank, of midnight weeds collected,
   With Hecate's° ban° thrice blasted, thrice infected,   270
   Thy natural magic and dire property°
   On wholesome life usurp° immediately.

[*He pours the poison into the sleeper's ears.*]

Hamlet. He poisons him i' the garden for's estate;°
   his name's Gonzago. The story is extant, and writ
   in choice Italian. You shall see anon how the   275
   murderer gets the love of Gonzago's wife.
Ophelia. The King rises.
Hamlet. What, frighted with false fire?°
Queen. How fares my lord?
Polonius. Give o'er the play.   280
King. Give me some light! Away!
All. Lights, lights, lights!

Exeunt all but HAMLET *and* HORATIO.

Hamlet.
   Why, let the stricken deer go weep,
   The hart ungalled° play;
   For some must watch, while some must sleep: 285
   Thus runs the world away.

---

268. **Confederate ... seeing:** the opportune moment, with no witnesses.
270. **Hecate:** goddess of sorcery. **ban:** curse.
271. **property:** nature.
272. **usurp:** take possession.
273. **estate:** kingdom.
278. **false fire:** firing blanks. (The murder of Gonzago is make-believe.)
284. **ungalled:** uninjured.

Would not this, sir, and a forest of feathers°—if
the rest of my fortunes turn Turk with me°—with
two Provincial roses° on my razed° shoes, get me a
fellowship in a cry° of players, sir?   290
Horatio. Half a share.
Hamlet. A whole one, I!
    For thou dost know, O Damon° dear,
      This realm dismantled was
      Of Jove himself; and now reigns here   295
      A very, very—pajock.°
Horatio. You might have rhymed.
Hamlet. O good Horatio, I'll take the ghost's word
for a thousand pound! Didst perceive?
Horatio. Very well, my lord.   300
Hamlet. Upon the talk of the poisoning?
Horatio. I did very well note him.
Hamlet. Aha! Come, some music! Come, the recorders!°
    For if the King like not the comedy,
    Why then, belike he likes it not, perdy.°   305
    Come, some music!

Enter ROSENCRANTZ *and* GUILDENSTERN.

Guildenstern. Good my lord, vouchsafe me a word
with you.
Hamlet. Sir, a whole history.
Guildenstern. The King, sir—   310
Hamlet. Ay, sir, what of him?

---

287. **forest of feathers:** plumes worn by actors.
288. **turn Turk with me:** turn against me.
289. **roses:** rosettes of ribbons (again, part of an actor's costume). **razed:** slashed.
290. **fellowship in a cry:** partnership in a troop.
293. **Damon:** In Greek legend, Damon and Pythias were loyal friends.
296. **pajock:** a contemptible fellow. (*Pajock* may also mean "peacock.")
303. **recorders:** wooden flutes.
305. **perdy:** by Jove (from the French *pardieu*).

Guildenstern. Is in his retirement, marvelous
distempered.°

Hamlet. With drink, sir?

Guildenstern. No, my lord; rather with choler.°   315

Hamlet. Your wisdom should show itself more richer
to signify this to his doctor; for, for me to put him
to his purgation° would perhaps plunge him into
far more choler.

Guildenstern. Good my lord, put your discourse into   320
some frame and start not so wildly from my affair.

Hamlet. I am tame, sir; pronounce.

Guildenstern. The Queen, your mother, in most great
affliction of spirit hath sent me to you.

Hamlet. You are welcome.   325

Guildenstern. Nay, good my lord, this courtesy is not
of the right breed.° If it shall please you to make
me a wholesome° answer, I will do your mother's
commandment; if not, your pardon° and my return
shall be the end of my business.   330

Hamlet. Sir, I cannot.

Guildenstern. What, my lord?

Hamlet. Make you a wholesome answer; my wit's
diseased. But, sir, such answer as I can make, you
shall command; or rather, as you say, my mother.   335
Therefore no more, but to the matter! My mother,
you say—

Rosencrantz. Then thus she says: your behavior
hath struck her into amazement and admiration.°

---

313. **distempered:** disturbed (but Hamlet picks up its other meaning:
"drunk").
315. **choler:** anger or bile. (Hamlet puns on these two meanings in lines
316–319.)
318. **purgation:** cleansing the body; also, purifying the soul.
327. **breed:** kind or sort; good manners (breeding).
328. **wholesome:** sane.
329. **pardon:** permission to leave.
339. **admiration:** astonishment.

Hamlet. O wonderful son, that can so astonish a   340
mother! But is there no sequel at the heels of this
mother's admiration? Impart.

Rosencrantz. She desires to speak with you in her
closet° ere you go to bed.

Hamlet. We shall obey, were she ten times our   345
mother. Have you any further trade° with us?

Rosencrantz. My lord, you once did love me.

Hamlet. So do still, by these pickers and stealers.°

Rosencrantz. Good my lord, what is your cause of
distemper? You do surely bar the door upon your   350
own liberty, if you deny your griefs to your friend.

Hamlet. Sir, I lack advancement.

Rosencrantz. How can that be, when you have the
voice of the King himself for your succession in
Denmark?   355

Hamlet. Ay, sir, but "while the grass grows"°—the
proverb is something musty.

Enter PLAYERS *with recorders.*

O, the recorders! Let me see one. To withdraw
with you—why do you go about to recover the
wind of me, as if you would drive me into a toil?°   360

Guildenstern. O my lord, if my duty be too bold, my
love is too unmannerly. °

Hamlet. I do not well understand that. Will you
play upon this pipe?°

---

344. **closet:** private room for meditation or conference.
346. **trade:** business.
348. **pickers and stealers:** hands (from the Anglican catechism, "To keep
my hands from picking and stealing").
356. **"while ... grows":** The proverb is "While the grass grows, the horse
starves."
359–60. **recover ... toil?:** get downwind so you can drive me into a net?
361–62. **if ... unmannerly:** if I seem too assertive, it is only because of my
love for you.
364. **pipe:** the recorder.

Guildenstern. My lord, I cannot.   365

Hamlet. I pray you.

Guildenstern. Believe me, I cannot.

Hamlet. I do beseech you.

Guildenstern. I know no touch of it, my lord.

Hamlet. It is as easy as lying. Govern these   370
ventages° with your fingers and thumb, give it
breath with your mouth, and it will discourse
most eloquent music. Look you, these are the
stops.°

Guildenstern. But these cannot I command to any   375
utt'rance of harmony. I have not the skill.

Hamlet. Why, look you now, how unworthy a thing
you make of me! You would play upon me; you
would seem to know my stops; you would pluck
out the heart of my mystery; you would sound me   380
from my lowest note to the top of my compass;°
and there is much music, excellent voice, in this
little organ,° yet cannot you make it speak.
'Sblood, do you think I am easier to be played on
than a pipe? Call me what instrument you will,   385
though you can fret° me, you cannot play upon me.

Enter POLONIUS.

God bless you, sir!

Polonius. My lord, the Queen would speak with
you, and presently.°

Hamlet. Do you see yonder cloud that's almost in   390
shape of a camel?

---

371. **ventages:** holes.
374. **stops:** finger holes.
381. **compass:** range.
383. **organ:** any musical instrument.
386. **fret:** a finger stop on a stringed instrument. (Hamlet puns on the
    double meaning of the word *fret*.)
389. **presently:** at once.

Polonius. By the mass, and 'tis like a camel
  indeed.
Hamlet. Methinks it is like a weasel.
Polonius. It is backed like a weasel.   395
Hamlet. Or like a whale.
Polonius. Very like a whale.
Hamlet. Then I will come to my mother by-and-by.
  —They fool me to the top of my bent.° —I will come
  by and by.   400
Polonius. I will say so.
Hamlet. "By-and-by" is easily said. —Leave me,
  friends.

                              Exeunt all but HAMLET.

  'Tis now the very witching time of night,
  When churchyards yawn, and hell itself breathes
     out   405
  Contagion to this world. Now could I drink hot blood
  And do such bitter business as the day
  Would quake to look on. Soft! now to my mother!
  O heart, lose not thy nature;° let not ever
  The soul of Nero enter this firm bosom.°   410
  Let me be cruel, not unnatural;
  I will speak daggers to her, but use none.
  My tongue and soul in this be hypocrites—
  How in my words somever she be shent,°
  To give them seals° never, my soul, consent!   415

                                  Exit.

---

399. **They ... bent:** They make me play the fool to the utmost.
409. **nature:** natural feeling.
410. **The ... bosom:** Nero (A.D. 37–68) put his mother, Agrippina, to death
      for poisoning her husband, the emperor Claudius.
414. **shent:** reproved.
415. **give them seals:** authorize them to take harsh action.

Scene 3. *A room in the castle.*

Enter KING CLAUDIUS, ROSENCRANTZ, *and* GUILDENSTERN.

King.
  I like him not, nor stands it safe with us
  To let his madness range. Therefore prepare you;
  I your commission will forthwith dispatch,°
  And he to England shall along with you.
  The terms of our estate° may not endure   5
  Hazard so near us as doth hourly grow
  Out of his lunacies.
Guildenstern.   We will ourselves provide.°
  Most holy and religious fear it is
  To keep those many many bodies safe
  That live and feed upon your Majesty.   10
Rosencrantz.
  The single and peculiar° life is bound
  With all the strength and armor of the mind
  To keep itself from noyance;° but much more
  That spirit upon whose weal° depends and rests
  The lives of many. The cease of majesty°   15
  Dies not alone, but like a gulf° doth draw
  What's near it with it. It is a massy wheel,
  Fixed on the summit of the highest mount,
  To whose huge spokes ten thousand lesser things
  Are mortised and adjoined; which when it falls,   20
  Each small annexment, petty consequence,
  Attends° the boist'rous ruin. Never alone
  Did the King sigh, but with a general groan.

III.3.3. **dispatch:** deal with.
5.   **The ... estate:** my position as king.
7.   **provide:** make ready.
11. **peculiar:** individual.
13. **noyance:** harm.
14. **weal:** well-being.
15. **cease of majesty:** death of a king.
16. **gulf:** whirlpool.
22. **Attends:** participates in.

King.

Arm you, I pray you, to° this speedy voyage;
For we will fetters put upon this fear,   25
Which now goes too free-footed.

Rosencrantz and Guildenstern.   We will haste us.

Exeunt ROSENCRANTZ *and* GUILDENSTERN.
Enter POLONIUS.

Polonius.

My lord, he's going to his mother's closet.
Behind the arras I'll convey myself
To hear the process.° I'll warrant she'll tax him home;°
And, as you said, and wisely was it said,   30
'Tis meet° that some more audience than a mother,
Since nature makes them partial, should o'erhear
The speech, of vantage.° Fare you well, my liege.
I'll call upon you ere you go to bed
And tell you what I know.

King.   Thanks, dear my lord.   35

Exit POLONIUS.

O, my offense is rank, it smells to heaven;
It hath the primal eldest curse upon't,
A brother's murder!° Pray can I not,
Though inclination be as sharp as will.
My stronger guilt defeats my strong intent,   40
And, like a man to double business bound,
I stand in pause where I shall first begin,
And both neglect. What if this cursed hand

---

24.   **Arm you ... to:** get ready for.
29.   **process:** proceedings. **tax him home:** take him to task (reprimand him).
31.   **meet:** suitable.
33.   **of vantage:** in addition (or, possibly, from a good vantage point).
37–38. **primal ... murder:** a reference to the account (in the Book of Genesis) of Cain's murder of his brother, Abel, and the curse God put upon Cain.

Were thicker than itself with brother's blood,
Is there not rain enough in the sweet heavens   45
To wash it white as snow? Whereto serves mercy
But to confront the visage of offense?°
And what's in prayer but this twofold force,
To be forestalled° ere we come to fall,
Or pardoned being down? Then I'll look up;   50
My fault is past. But, O, what form of prayer
Can serve my turn? "Forgive me my foul murder"?
That cannot be; since I am still possessed
Of those effects° for which I did the murder—
My crown, mine own ambition, and my queen.   55
May one be pardoned and retain the offense?°
In the corrupted currents° of this world
Offense's gilded° hand may shove by° justice,
And oft 'tis seen the wicked prize itself
Buys out the law; but 'tis not so above.°   60
There is no shuffling;° there the action lies
In his true nature,° and we ourselves compelled,
Even to the teeth and forehead° of our faults,
To give in evidence. What then? What rests?
Try what repentance can. What can it not?   65
Yet what can it when one can not repent?
O wretched state! O bosom black as death!
O limed° soul, that, struggling to be free,

---

47.   **confront ... offense:** look the crime in the face.
49.   **forestalled:** prevented.
54.   **effects:** gains, profits.
56.   **offense:** gains.
57.   **corrupted currents:** evil ways.
58.   **gilded:** gold-covered. **shove by:** push aside.
60.   **above:** in heaven.
61.   **shuffling:** evasion or trickery.
61–62. **the action ... nature:** the case is tried on its own merits.
63.   **teeth and forehead:** face-to-face confrontation.
68.   **limed:** snared (like a bird caught in sticky birdlime).

Art more engaged!° Help, angels! Make assay.°
Bow, stubborn knees; and heart with strings of steel,   70
Be soft as sinews of the new-born babe!
All may be well.

Retires and kneels.
Enter HAMLET.

Hamlet.
Now might I do it pat,° now he is praying;
And now I'll do't. And so he goes to heaven,
And so am I revenged. That would be scanned.°   75
A villain kills my father; and for that,
I, his sole son, do this same villain send
To heaven.
Why, this is hire and salary, not revenge!
He took my father grossly, full of bread,°   80
With all his crimes broad blown,° as flush° as May;
And how his audit° stands, who knows save heaven?
But in our circumstance° and course of thought,
'Tis heavy with him; and am I then revenged,
To take him in the purging of his soul,   85
When he is fit and seasoned° for his passage?
No.
Up, sword, and know thou a more horrid hent.°
When he is drunk asleep; or in his rage;
Or in the incestuous pleasure of his bed;   • 90
At gaming, swearing, or about some act
That has no relish° of salvation in't—

---

69.   **engaged:** entangled. **assay:** an attempt.
73.   **pat:** opportunely.
75.   **That ... scanned:** That should be looked into carefully.
80.   **grossly ... bread:** full of sensual pleasure and not in a state of grace.
81.   **broad blown:** in full bloom. **flush:** full of life.
82.   **audit:** account (of his good deeds and his sins).
83.   **in our circumstance:** from our point of view.
86.   **seasoned:** made ready.
88.   **hent:** opportunity.
92.   **relish:** flavor.

Then trip him, that his heels may kick at heaven,
And that his soul may be as damned and black
As hell, whereto it goes. My mother stays.°   95
This physic° but prolongs thy sickly days.

Exit.

King. [*Rises.*]
My words fly up, my thoughts remain below;
Words without thoughts never to heaven go.

Exit.

Scene 4. *The Queen's closet.*

Enter QUEEN GERTRUDE *and* POLONIUS.

Polonius.
He will come straight. Look you lay home to him.
Tell him his pranks have been too broad° to bear
   with,
And that your Grace hath screened and stood
   between
Much heat and him. I'll silence me° even here.
Pray you be round° with him.   5
Hamlet. [*Within.*] Mother, mother, mother!
Queen. I'll warrant you; fear me not.
Withdraw, I hear him coming.

POLONIUS *hides behind the arras.*
Enter HAMLET.

Hamlet.
Now, mother, what's the matter?

---

95.   **stays:** is waiting.
96.   **physic:** purging (here, the king's prayer).
III.4.2. **broad:** unrestrained.
4.   **silence me:** say no more.
5.   **round:** outspoken.

Queen.
Hamlet, thou hast thy father much offended.   10
Hamlet.
Mother, you have my father much offended.
Queen.
Come, come, you answer with an idle° tongue.
Hamlet.
Go, go, you question with a wicked tongue.
Queen.
Why, how now, Hamlet!
Hamlet.   What's the matter now?
Queen.
Have you forgot me?°
Hamlet.   No, by the rood,° not so!   15
You are the Queen, your husband's brother's wife.°
And—would it were not so—you are my mother.
Queen.
Nay, then, I'll set those to you that can speak.
Hamlet.
Come, come, and sit you down, you shall not budge!
You go not till I set you up a glass°   20
Where you may see the inmost part of you.
Queen.
What wilt thou do? Thou wilt not murder me?
Help, help, ho!
Polonius. [*Behind.*] What, ho! help, help, help!
Hamlet. [*Draws.*]
How now! a rat? Dead for a ducat,° dead!   25

Makes a pass through the arras and kills POLONIUS.

---

12.   **idle:** foolish.
15.   **forgot me:** forgotten who I am. **by the rood:** by the cross.
16.   **husband's brother's wife:** a reminder of the ban against a woman
      marrying the brother of her husband.
20.   **glass:** mirror.
25.   **ducat:** a gold coin (Hamlet may be betting a ducat that Polonius is
      dead; more likely he is implying that it cost little effort to kill this
      person, who Hamlet thought was Claudius).

Polonius. [*Behind.*]
  O, I am slain!
Queen.   O me, what hast thou done?
Hamlet.
  Nay, I know not. Is it the King?
Queen.
  O, what a rash and bloody deed is this!
Hamlet.
  A bloody deed—almost as bad, good mother,
  As kill a king, and marry with his brother.   30
Queen.
  As kill a king?
Hamlet.   Ay, lady, 'twas my word.

Lifts up the arras and discovers POLONIUS.

  Thou wretched, rash, intruding fool, farewell!
  I took thee for thy better. Take thy fortune.
  Thou find'st to be too busy is some danger—
  Leave wringing of your hands. Peace! sit you down   35
  And let me wring your heart; for so I shall
  If it be made of penetrable stuff;
  If damned custom° have not brazed it so°
  That it is proof and bulwark against sense.
Queen.
  What have I done, that thou dar'st wag thy tongue   40
  In noise so rude against me?
Hamlet.   Such an act
  That blurs the grace and blush of modesty;
  Calls virtue hypocrite; takes off the rose°
  From the fair forehead of an innocent love,
  And sets a blister° there; makes marriage vows   45
  As false as dicers' oaths. O, such a deed

---

38. **custom:** habit. **brazed it:** hardened it into brass.
43. **rose:** The rose was the emblem of love.
45. **blister:** the result of being branded as a whore.

As from the body of contraction° plucks
The very soul, and sweet religion makes
A rhapsody of words! Heaven's face doth glow;
Yea, this solidity and compound mass,°   50
With tristful° visage, as against the doom,°
Is thought-sick at the act.

Queen.   Ay me, what act,
That roars so loud, and thunders in the index?°

Hamlet.
Look here, upon this picture, and on this,
The counterfeit presentment of two brothers.   55
See what a grace was seated on this brow;
Hyperion's curls; the front° of Jove himself;
An eye like Mars, to threaten and command;
A station° like the herald Mercury°
New lighted° on a heaven-kissing hill: 60
A combination and a form indeed
Where every god did seem to set his seal
To give the world assurance of a man.
This was your husband. Look you now what follows.
Here is your husband, like a mildewed ear   65
Blasting° his wholesome brother. Have you eyes?
Could you on this fair mountain leave° to feed,
And batten° on this moor? Ha! have you eyes?
You cannot call it love; for at your age

---

47.   **contraction:** the making of solemn contracts such as the marriage
       contract.
50.   **solidity ... mass:** the world.
51.   **tristful:** sad. **as ... doom:** as if thinking of Judgment Day. (The world
       grows sick at the thought of Gertrude's deed.)
53.   **That ... index:** that receives so violent an introduction.
57.   **front:** forehead.
59.   **station:** stance. **Mercury:** the messenger of the Roman gods.
60.   **New lighted:** having just arrived. (Artists often portrayed Mercury
       this way.)
66.   **Blasting:** destroying.
67.   **leave:** cease.
68.   **batten:** feed gluttonously.

The heyday° in the blood is tame, it's humble,   70
And waits upon° the judgment; and what judgment
Would step from this to this? Sense° sure you have,
Else could you not have motion; but sure that sense
Is apoplexed;° for madness would not err,
Nor sense to ecstasy° was ne'er so thralled°   75
But it reserved some quantity of choice
To serve in such a difference.° What devil was't
That thus hath cozened you at hoodman-blind?°
Eyes without feeling, feeling without sight,
Ears without hands or eyes, smelling sans all,   80
Or but a sickly part of one true sense
Could not so mope.
O shame! where is thy blush? Rebellious hell,
If thou canst mutiny in a matron's bones,
To flaming youth let virtue be as wax   85
And melt in her own fire.° Proclaim no shame
When the compulsive ardor gives the charge,
Since frost° itself as actively doth burn,
And reason panders will.°

Queen.   O Hamlet, speak no more!
Thou turn'st mine eyes into my very soul,   90
And there I see such black and grained° spots
As will not leave their tint.

---

70.   **heyday:** excitement.
71.   **waits upon:** is subordinate to.
72.   **Sense:** the senses.
74.   **apoplexed:** paralyzed.
75.   **ecstasy:** passion. **thralled:** enslaved.
76–77. **But ... difference:** but it retained some small ability to choose
      between alternatives.
78.   **cozened ... blind:** cheated you at blind-man's-bluff.
83–86. **Rebellious ... fire:** If hellish lust can overthrow virtue even in a
      mature woman, then virtue doesn't stand a chance in hotblooded
      youth.
88.   **frost:** numbed passion.
89.   **reason ... will:** One finds reasons to indulge one's base desires
      instead of curbing them.
91.   **grained:** permanent, ingrained.

Hamlet.   Nay, but to live
   In the rank sweat of an enseamed° bed,
   Stewed° in corruption, honeying and making love
   Over the nasty sty!
Queen.   O, speak to me no more!   95
   These words, like daggers, enter in mine ears.
   No more, sweet Hamlet!
Hamlet.   A murderer and a villain!
   A slave that is not twentieth part the tithe°
   Of your precedent lord; a vice° of kings;
   A cutpurse° of the empire and the rule,   100
   That from a shelf the precious diadem stole
   And put it in his pocket!
Queen.   No more!

Enter GHOST.

Hamlet.
   A king of shreds and patches—
   Save me and hover o'er me with your wings,
   You heavenly guards! What would your gracious
      figure?   105
Queen.
   Alas, he's mad!
Hamlet.
   Do you not come your tardy son to chide,
   That, lapsed in time and passion, lets go by
   The important acting of your dread command?
   O, say!   110
Ghost.
   Do not forget. This visitation
   Is but to whet thy almost blunted purpose.

---

93. **enseamed:** grease-soaked.
94. **Stewed:** bathed (with a pun on *stew,* meaning "brothel").
98. **the tithe:** one tenth.
99. **vice:** a character in medieval drama representing both evil and clownishness.
100. **cutpurse:** pickpocket.

But look, amazement on thy mother sits.
O, step between her and her fighting soul!
Conceit° in weakest bodies strongest works.   115
Speak to her, Hamlet.
Hamlet.   How is it with you, lady?
Queen. Alas, how is't with you,
    That you do bend your eye on vacancy,
    And with the incorporal° air do hold discourse?
    Forth at your eyes your spirits wildly peep;   120
    And, as the sleeping soldiers in the alarm,
    Your bedded hairs,° like life in excrements,°
    Start up, and stand on end. O gentle son,
    Upon the heat and flame of thy distemper
    Sprinkle cool patience! Whereon do you look?   125
Hamlet.
    On him, on him! Look you how pale he glares!
    His form and cause conjoined, preaching to stones,
    Would make them capable.°—Do not look upon me,
    Lest with this piteous action you convert°
    My stern effects.° Then what I have to do   130
    Will want true color°—tears perchance for blood.
Queen.
    To whom do you speak this?
Hamlet.   Do you see nothing there?
Queen.
    Nothing at all; yet all that is I see.
Hamlet.
    Nor did you nothing hear?
Queen.   No, nothing but ourselves.

---

115. **Conceit:** imagination.
119. **incorporal:** bodiless.
122. **bedded hair:** hair lying flat. **excrements:** outgrowths.
128. **capable:** able to respond emotionally.
129. **convert:** divert.
130. **effects:** deeds.
131. **want true color:** lack proper character.

Hamlet.

 Why, look you there! Look how it steals away!   135
 My father, in his habit as he lived!°
 Look where he goes even now out at the portal!

            Exit GHOST.

Queen.

 This the very coinage of your brain.
 This bodiless creation ecstasy°
 Is very cunning in.
Hamlet.   Ecstasy?   140
 My pulse as yours doth temperately keep time
 And makes as healthful music. It is not madness
 That I have utt'red. Bring me to the test,
 And I the matter will reword; which madness
 Would gambol° from. Mother, for love of grace, 145
 Lay not that flattering unction° to your soul,
 That not your trespass but my madness speaks.
 It will but skin° and film the ulcerous place,
 Whilst rank corruption, mining° all within,
 Infects unseen. Confess yourself to heaven;   150
 Repent what's past; avoid what is to come;
 And do not spread the compost° on the weeds
 To make them ranker. Forgive me this my virtue;
 For in the fatness of these pursy° times
 Virtue itself of vice must pardon beg—   155
 Yea, curb° and woo for leave to do him good.

---

136. **his ... lived:** the costume that he wore when he was alive.
139. **ecstasy:** madness.
145. **gambol:** leap.
146. **Lay ... unction:** Do not apply that soothing ointment.
148. **skin:** grow skin.
149. **mining:** undermining.
152. **compost:** fertilizer made of decaying organic matter.
154. **pursy:** flabby, bloated.
156. **curb:** bow.

Queen.
> O Hamlet, thou hast cleft my heart in twain.°
Hamlet. O, throw away the worser part of it,
> And live the purer with the other half.
> Good night—but go not to mine uncle's bed.   160
> Assume° a virtue, if you have it not.
> That monster, custom, who all sense doth eat
> Of habits evil, is angel yet in this,
> That to the use of actions fair and good
> He likewise gives a frock or livery,   165
> That aptly is put on.° Refrain tonight,
> And that shall lend a kind of easiness
> To the next abstinence; the next more easy;
> For use almost can change the stamp of nature,
> And either ...° the devil, or throw him out   170
> With wondrous potency. Once more, good night;
> And when you are desirous to be blest,
> I'll blessing beg of you. —For this same lord,
> I do repent; but heaven hath pleased it so,
> To punish me with this, and this with me,   175
> That I must be their scourge and minister.°
> I will bestow° him, and will answer° well
> The death I gave him. So again, good night.
> I must be cruel, only to be kind;
> Thus bad begins and worse remains behind.°   180
> One word more, good lady.
Queen.   What shall I do?
Hamlet.
> Not this, by no means, that I bid you do:

---

157. **in twain:** divided between regret for her sins and loyalty to
>   Claudius.
161. **Assume:** adopt.
162–66. **who ... on:** which destroys our sense of doing evil because we
>   become hardened by habit, also creates good habits.
170. The missing word usually supplied here is *master* or *lodge*.
176. **their ... minister:** heaven's instrument of punishment.
177. **bestow:** dispose of. **answer:** atone for.
180. **remains behind:** is still to come.

Let the bloat King tempt you again to bed;
Pinch wanton° on your cheek; call you his mouse;
And let him, for a pair° of reechy° kisses,   185
Or paddling° in your neck with his damned fingers,
Make you to ravel all this matter out,
That I essentially am not in madness,
But mad in craft. 'Twere good you let him know;
For who, that's but a queen, fair, sober, wise,   190
Would from a paddock,° from a bat, a gib,°
Such dear concernings° hide? Who would do so?
No, in despite of sense and secrecy,
Unpeg the basket on the house's top,
Let the birds fly, and like the famous ape,   195
To try conclusions, in the basket creep,
And break your own neck down.°

Queen.
Be thou assured, if words be made of breath,
And breath of life, I have no life to breathe
What thou hast said to me.   200

Hamlet.
I must to England; you know that?

Queen.   Alack,
I had forgot. 'Tis so concluded on.

Hamlet.
There's letters sealed; and my two schoolfellows,
Whom I will trust as I will adders fanged,
They bear the mandate;° they must sweep my way,°   205

---

184. **Pinch wanton:** leave pinch marks that proclaim you to be a wanton.
185. **pair:** few. **reechy:** foul.
186. **paddling:** fondling.
191. **paddock:** toad. **gib:** (pronounced with a hard *g*) tomcat. (Cats were notorious for being witches' familiars).
192. **Such ... concernings:** matters that are so important.
195–97. **like ... down:** an allusion to a story (now lost) about an ape that saw birds flying out of a basket on a rooftop. Thinking that he could fly by getting into the birds' basket, he fell off the roof to his death.
205. **mandate:** command. **sweep my way:** escort me.

And marshal me to knavery.° Let it work;
For 'tis the sport to have the engineer
Hoist with his own petar;° and 't shall go hard
But I will delve one yard below their mines
And blow them at the moon. O, 'tis most sweet   210
When in one line two crafts directly meet.°
This man shall set me packing.°
I'll lug the guts into the neighbor room.
—Mother, good night. —Indeed this counselor
Is now most still, most secret, and most grave,   215
Who was in life a foolish prating knave.
Come, sir, to draw toward an end° with you.
Good night, mother.

       Exeunt separately, HAMLET *dragging* POLONIUS.

---

206.   **marshal ... knavery:** lead me while they do wrong.
207–08. **the engineer ... petar:** the demolitions expert blown up by his own
      bomb.
211.   **in ... meet:** two crafty schemes on a collision course.
212.   **packing:** off in a hurry (but with a second meaning of "plotting").
217.   **draw ... end:** finish my business.

Act IV

Scene 1. *A room in the castle.*

Enter KING CLAUDIUS, QUEEN GERTRUDE, ROSENCRANTZ, *and*
GUILDENSTERN.

King.
There's matter in these sighs. These profound° heaves
You must translate; 'tis fit we understand them.
Where is your son?
Queen.
Bestow this place on us a little while.

                 Exeunt ROSENCRANTZ *and* GUILDENSTERN.

Ah, mine own lord, what have I seen tonight!   5
King.
What, Gertrude? How does Hamlet?
Queen.
Mad as the sea and wind when both contend
Which is the mightier. In his lawless fit,
Behind the arras hearing something stir,
Whips out his rapier, cries "A rat, a rat!"   10
And in this brainish apprehension° kills
The unseen good old man.
King.   O heavy deed!
It had been so with us, had we° been there.
His liberty is full of threats to all—
To you yourself, to us, to every one.   15
Alas, how shall this bloody deed be answered?
It will be laid to us, whose providence°

IV.1.1. **profound:** The first syllable is stressed here.
11.   **brainish apprehension:** insane imagining.
13.   **us … we:** Again, the royal *we*. Read *us* as "me," and *we* as "I."
17.   **providence:** foresight.

Should have kept short,° restrained, and out of
  haunt°
This mad young man. But so much was our love
We would not understand what was most fit,   20
But, like the owner of a foul disease,
To keep it from divulging,° let it feed
Even on the pith of life. Where is he gone?

Queen

To draw apart the body he hath killed,
O'er whom his very madness, like some ore°   25
Among a mineral° of metals base,
Shows itself pure. He weeps for what is done.

King.

O Gertrude, come away!
The sun no sooner shall the mountains touch,
But we will ship him hence; and this vile deed   30
We must with all our majesty and skill
Both countenance° and excuse. Ho, Guildenstern!

Enter ROSENCRANTZ *and* GUILDENSTERN.

Friends both, go join you with some further aid.
Hamlet in madness hath Polonius slain,
And from his mother's closet hath he dragged him. 35
Go seek him out; speak fair, and bring the body
Into the chapel. I pray you haste in this.

Exeunt ROSENCRANTZ *and* GUILDENSTERN.

Come, Gertrude, we'll call up our wisest friends
And let them know both what we mean to do
And what's untimely done. ....°   40

---

18. **short:** on a short leash. **out of haunt:** away from others.
22. **divulging:** being made known.
25. **ore:** precious metal.
26. **mineral:** mine.
32. **countenance:** sanction.
40. There is a gap in the text. Most editions accept the addition of the
     words "So, haply, slander."

Whose whisper o'er the world's diameter,
As level as the cannon to his blank,
Transports his pois'ned shot—may miss our name
And hit the woundless° air.—O, come away!
My soul is full of discord and dismay.   45

                                        Exeunt.

Scene 2. *Another room in the castle.*

Enter HAMLET.

Hamlet. Safely stowed.
Rosencrantz and Guildenstern. [*Within.*] Hamlet!
   Lord Hamlet!
Hamlet. But soft! What noise? Who calls on
   Hamlet? O, here they come.   5

Enter ROSENCRANTZ *and* GUILDENSTERN.

Rosencrantz. What have you done, my lord, with
   the dead body?
Hamlet.
   Compounded it with dust, whereto 'tis kin.°
Rosencrantz.
   Tell us where 'tis, that we may take it thence
   And bear it to the chapel.   10
Hamlet. Do not believe it.
Rosencrantz. Believe what?
Hamlet. That I can keep your counsel,° and not mine

---

44.   **woundless:** invulnerable.
IV.2.8. Compounded ... kin: an allusion to Genesis, the first book of the
   Bible: "Dust thou art, and unto dust shalt thou return."
13.   **counsel:** secret. (Hamlet reminds them of his promise to keep secret
   his knowledge that they were summoned to Denmark by Claudius.)

own. Besides, to be demanded of a sponge, what
replication should be made by the son of a king?   15
Rosencrantz. Take you me for a sponge, my lord?
Hamlet. Ay, sir, that soaks up the King's
   countenance,° his rewards, his authorities.° But
   such officers do the King best service in the end.
   He keeps them, like an ape, in the corner of his   20
   jaw; first mouthed, to be last swallowed. When
   he needs what you have gleaned, it is but
   squeezing you and, sponge, you shall be dry again.
Rosencrantz. I understand you not, my lord.
Hamlet. I am glad of it: a knavish speech sleeps in   25
   a foolish ear.
Rosencrantz. My lord, you must tell us where the
   body is and go with us to the King.
Hamlet. The body is with the King, but the King is
   not with the body. The King is a thing—   30
Guildenstern. A thing, my lord?
Hamlet. Of nothing.° Bring me to him. Hide fox,
   and all after.°

Exeunt.

Scene 3. *Another room in the castle.*

Enter KING CLAUDIUS.

King.
   I have sent to seek him and to find the body.
   How dangerous is it that this man goes loose!
   Yet must not we put the strong law on him.
   He's loved of the distracted° multitude,

---

18.   **countenance:** favor. **authorities:** influence.
30–32. The King … nothing: Hamlet implies that the king is worthless.
32–33. Hide … after: a catch phrase used in a game like hide-and-seek.
IV. 3.4. distracted: confused, senseless.

Who like not in their judgment, but their eyes;   5
And where 'tis so, the offender's scourge° is weighed,
But never the offense. To bear° all smooth and even,
This sudden sending him away must seem
Deliberate pause.° Diseases desperate grown
By desperate appliance are relieved,°   10
Or not at all.

Enter ROSENCRANTZ.

          How now! what hath befall'n?
Rosencrantz.
Where the dead body is bestowed, my lord,
We cannot get from him.
King.   But where is he?
Rosencrantz.
Without,° my lord; guarded, to know your pleasure.
King.
Bring him before us.
Rosencrantz.   Ho, Guildenstern! Bring in my
   lord.   15

Enter HAMLET, GUILDENSTERN, *and* ATTENDANTS.

King. Now, Hamlet, where's Polonius?
Hamlet. At supper.
King. At supper? Where?
Hamlet. Not where he eats, but where he is eaten.
A certain convocation of politic worms° are e'en°   20
at him. Your worm is your only emperor for diet.
We fat all creatures else to fat us, and we fat

---

6.   **scourge:** punishment.
7.   **bear:** carry out.
9.   **Deliberate pause:** careful consideration.
9–10. **Diseases ... relieved:** an allusion to the proverb that desperate diseases require desperate remedies.
14.   **Without:** outside.
20.   **convocation ... worms:** probably a reference to the Diet of Worms, convened in 1521 by the Emperor of the Holy Roman Empire. **e'en:** even now.

ourselves for maggots. Your fat king and your lean
beggar is but variable service°—two dishes, but to
one table. That's the end.   25

King. Alas, alas!

Hamlet. A man may fish with the worm that hath
eat of a king, and eat of the fish that hath fed of
that worm.

King. What dost thou mean by this?   30

Hamlet. Nothing but to show you how a king may go
a progress° through the guts of a beggar.

King. Where is Polonius?

Hamlet. In heaven. Send thither to see. If your
messenger find him not there, seek him i' the other   35
place yourself. But indeed, if you find him not
within this month, you shall nose him as you go
up the stairs into the lobby.

King. [*To* ATTENDANTS.] Go seek him there.

Hamlet. He will stay till ye come.   40

Exeunt ATTENDANTS.

King.
  Hamlet, this deed, for thine especial safety,—
  Which we do tender° as we dearly° grieve
  For that which thou hast done,—must send thee hence
  With fiery quickness. Therefore prepare thyself.
  The bark° is ready and the wind at help,   45
  The associates tend,° and every thing is bent°
  For England.

Hamlet.   For England?

King.   Ay, Hamlet.

Hamlet.   Good.

---

24. **variable service:** different courses.
32. **progress:** state journey that a monarch makes through his or her
    realm.
42. **tender:** have regard for. **dearly:** deeply.
45. **bark:** ship.
46. **tend:** wait. **bent:** curved like a bow ready to discharge an arrow.

King.
> So is it, if thou knew'st our purposes.

Hamlet. I see a cherub that sees them.° But come,
> for England! Farewell, dear mother.   50

King. Thy loving father, Hamlet.

Hamlet. My mother! Father and mother is man and
> wife; man and wife is one flesh; and so, my mother.
> Come, for England.

Exit.

King.
> Follow him at foot;° tempt him with speed aboard;   55
> Delay it not, I'll have him hence tonight.
> Away! for everything is sealed and done
> That else leans on the affair.° Pray you make haste.

Exeunt ROSENCRANTZ *and* GUILDENSTERN.

> And, England,° if my love thou hold'st at aught,°—
> As my great power thereof may give thee sense,°   60
> Since yet thy cicatrice looks raw and red
> After the Danish sword, and thy free awe
> Pays homage to us—thou mayst not coldly set
> Our sovereign process,° which imports at full,°
> By letters congruing to that effect,   65
> The present° death of Hamlet. Do it, England;
> For like the hectic in my blood he rages,
> And thou must cure me. Till I know 'tis done,

---

49.   **I ... them:** Since cherubs were thought to be all-knowing, Hamlet
        hints that he knows what the king is up to.
55.   **at foot:** close behind.
58.   **leans ... affair:** pertains to the business.
59.   **England:** King of England. **hold'st at aught:** value at all.
60.   **give thee sense:** cause you to value my friendship.
63–64. **coldly ... process:** regard slightly our royal command.
64.   **imports at full:** conveys full direction for.
66.   **present:** immediate.

Howe'er my haps,° my joys were ne'er begun.

Exit.

Scene 4. *A plain in Denmark.*

Enter FORTINBRAS, *a* CAPTAIN, *and* SOLDIERS, *marching.*

Fortinbras.
Go, Captain, from me greet the Danish King.
Tell him that by his license Fortinbras
Craves the conveyance of° a promised march
Over his kingdom. You know the rendezvous.
If that his Majesty would aught with us,   5
We shall express our duty in his eye;°
And let him know so.
Captain.   I will do't, my lord.
Fortinbras. Go softly° on.

                    Exeunt FORTINBRAS *and* SOLDIERS.
Enter HAMLET, ROSENCRANTZ, GUILDENSTERN, *and others.*

Hamlet.
Good sir, whose powers° are these?
Captain.
They are of Norway, sir.   10
Hamlet.
How purposed, sir, I pray you?
Captain.
Against some part of Poland.
Hamlet.
Who commands them, sir?

---

69.   **Howe'er my haps:** howsoever my fortune turns.
IV.4.3. **conveyance of:** escort for.
6.   **express ... eye:** pay our respects in his presence.
8.   **softly:** slowly.
9.   **powers:** troops.

Captain.
The nephew to old Norway, Fortinbras.
Hamlet.
Goes it against the main° of Poland, sir,   15
Or for some frontier?
Captain.
Truly to speak, and with no addition,°
We go to gain a little patch of ground
That hath in it no profit but the name.
To pay five ducats, five, I would not farm° it;   20
Nor will it yield to Norway or the Pole
A ranker° rate, should it be sold in fee.°
Hamlet.
Why, then the Polack never will defend it.
Captain.
Yes, it is already garrisoned.
Hamlet.
Two thousand souls and twenty thousand ducats   25
Will not debate° the question of this straw.
This is the imposthume° of much wealth and peace,
That inward breaks, and shows no cause without
Why the man dies. —I humbly thank you, sir.
Captain.
God be wi' you, sir.

                                                    Exit.

Rosencrantz.   Wilt please you go, my lord?   30
Hamlet.
I'll be with you straight. Go a little before.

                                    Exeunt all but HAMLET.

---

15. **main:** main part.
17. **addition:** embellishment.
20. **farm:** rent.
22. **ranker:** higher. **in fee:** outright.
26. **debate:** settle.
27. **imposthume:** abcess.

How all occasions do inform against me
And spur my dull° revenge! What is a man,
If his chief good and market° of his time
Be but to sleep and feed? A beast, no more.   35
Sure he that made us with such large discourse,°
Looking before and after,° gave us not
That capability and godlike reason
To fust° in us unused. Now, whether it be
Bestial oblivion, or some craven scruple   40
Of° thinking too precisely on the event°—
A thought which, quartered, hath but one part wisdom
And ever three parts coward—I do not know
Why yet I live to say "This thing's to do,"
Sith° I have cause, and will, and strength, and means   45
To do't. Examples gross as earth° exhort me.
Witness this army of such mass and charge,°
Led by a delicate and tender prince,
Whose spirit, with divine ambition puffed,
Makes mouths at the invisible event,°   50
Exposing what is mortal and unsure
To all that fortune, death, and danger dare,
Even for an eggshell. Rightly to be great
Is not to stir without great argument,
But greatly to find quarrel in a straw   55
When honor's at the stake.° How stand I then,

---

33.   **dull:** sluggish.
34.   **good and market:** advantage and use.
36.   **large discourse:** great ability to reason.
37.   **Looking ... after:** able to judge the past and look toward the future.
39.   **fust:** grow musty.
41.   **Of:** from. **event:** outcome.
45.   **Sith:** since.
46.   **gross as earth:** as obvious as the earth.
47.   **charge:** expense.
50.   **Makes ... event:** makes mocking faces at the unforeseeable outcome.
53–56. **Rightly ... stake:** The general meaning is "There is no greatness in
       holding back from taking action without provocation, but when
       honor is at stake, there is greatness in taking action even over a trifle."

That have a father killed, a mother stained,
Excitements of my reason and my blood,
And let all sleep? while, to my shame, I see
The imminent death of twenty thousand men   60
That for a fantasy° and trick° of fame
Go to their graves like beds, fight for a plot
Whereon the numbers cannot try the cause,°
Which is not tomb enough and continent°
To hide the slain? O, from this time forth,   65
My thoughts be bloody, or be nothing worth!

Exit.

Scene 5. *Elsinore. A room in the castle.*

Enter QUEEN GERTRUDE, HORATIO, *and a* GENTLEMAN.

Queen.
    I will not speak with her.
Gentleman.
    She is importunate,° indeed distract;°
    Her mood° will needs be pitied.
Queen.   What would she have?
Gentleman.
    She speaks much of her father; says she hears
    There's tricks° i' the world, and hems,° and beats her
        heart;   5
    Spurns enviously at straws;° speaks things in doubt,°
    That carry but half sense. Her speech is nothing,

---

61.   **fantasy:** illusion. **trick:** trifle.
63.   **Whereon ... cause:** not large enough to hold all those involved.
64.   **continent:** container.
IV.5.2. **importunate:** insistent. **distract:** insane.
3.   **mood:** state of mind.
5.   **tricks:** trickery. **hems:** makes sounds in her throat.
6.   **Spurns ... straws:** objects angrily to insignificant matters. **in doubt:**
       without much meaning.

Yet the unshaped use of it doth move
The hearers to collection; they aim at it,
And botch the words up fit to their own thoughts;   10
Which, as her winks and nods and gestures
   yield them,
Indeed would make one think there might be thought,
Though nothing sure, yet much unhappily.°

Horatio.
   'Twere good she were spoken with; for she may strew
   Dangerous conjectures in ill-breeding° minds.   15

Queen.
   Let her come in.

                                    Exit GENTLEMAN.

   [*Aside.*] To my sick soul (as sin's true nature is)°
   Each toy seems prologue to some great amiss.
   So full of artless jealousy is guilt
   It spills itself in fearing to be spilt.   20

Enter OPHELIA, *distracted.*

Ophelia.
   Where is the beauteous Majesty of Denmark?
Queen. How now, Ophelia?
Ophelia. [*Sings.*]
     How should I your true-love know
       From another one?
     By his cockle hat° and staff   25
       And his sandal shoon.°

7–13. Her ... unhappily: She makes no sense, yet her incoherence leads
    people to make inferences.
15.   **ill-breeding:** mischief-making.
17.   **soul ... is:** Gertrude sees sin as a disease of the soul. Hamlet's
    reproaches have done their work.
25.   **cockle hat:** A cockleshell in a hatband shows that the wearer is
    returning from a pilgrimage to the shrine of Saint James of
    Compostela, one of the twelve Christian apostles. Fictional lovers
    were often portrayed as going on pilgrimages.
26.   **shoon:** shoes. (Sandals and staff are also emblems of a pilgrim.)

Queen.
Alas, sweet lady, what imports this song?
Ophelia. Say you? Nay, pray you mark. [*Sings.*]
> He is dead and gone, lady,
>> He is dead and gone;   30
> At his head a grass-green turf,
>> At his heels a stone.

O, ho!
Queen. Nay, but Ophelia—
Ophelia. Pray you mark. [*Sings.*]   35
> White his shroud as the mountain snow—

[*Enter* KING CLAUDIUS.]

Queen. Alas, look here, my lord!
Ophelia. [*Sings.*]
>> Larded° all with sweet flowers;
>> Which bewept to the grave did not go
>>> With true-love showers.°   40
King. How do you, pretty lady?
Ophelia. Well, God 'ild° you! They say the owl was
a baker's daughter.° Lord, we know what we are,
but know not what we may be. God be at your table!
King. Conceit upon her father.   45
Ophelia. Pray let's have no words of this; but when
they ask you what it means, say you this: [*Sings.*]
>> Tomorrow is Saint Valentine's day,°
>>> All in the morning betime,
>> And I a maid at your window,   50
>>> To be your Valentine.

---

38.   **Larded:** strewn.
40.   **true-love showers:** the tears of his faithful love.
42.   **'ild:** reward (a corruption of the word *yield*).
42–43. **owl ... daughter:** A legend tells of a baker's daughter who refused
      Jesus the bread he asked for and so was turned into an owl.
48.   **Saint ... day:** Traditionally, the first unmarried man seen by an
      unmarried woman on February 14 is to be her husband.

> Then up he rose, and donned his clo'es,
>   And dupped° the chamber-door,
> Let in the maid, that out a maid
>   Never departed more.   55

King. Pretty Ophelia!

Ophelia. Indeed, la, without an oath, I'll make an
end on't: [*Sings.*]

> By Gis° and by Saint Charity,
>   Alack, and fie for shame!   60
> Young men will do't if they come to't,
>   By Cock,° they are to blame.
> Quoth she, "Before you tumbled me,
>   You promised me to wed."

He answers: 65

> "So would I ha' done, by yonder sun,
> An thou hadst not come to my bed."

King. How long hath she been thus?

Ophelia. I hope all will be well. We must be patient;
but I cannot choose but weep, to think they would   70
lay him i' the cold ground. My brother shall know
of it; and so I thank you for your good counsel.
Come, my coach! Good night, ladies. Good night,
sweet ladies. Good night, good night.

Exit.

King.

Follow her close;° give her good watch, I pray you.   75

Exit HORATIO.

O, this is the poison of deep grief; it springs
All from her father's death. O Gertrude, Gertrude,

---

53. **dupped:** opened.
58. **Gis:** substitute for the name Jesus (as *gee* is in modern English).
62. **Cock:** substitute for "God."
75. **close:** closely.

When sorrows come, they come not single spies,°
But in battalions! First, her father slain;
Next, your son gone, and he most violent author°   80
Of his own just remove; the people muddied,°
Thick and unwholesome in their thoughts and whispers
For good Polonius' death, and we have done but greenly
In hugger-mugger to inter him;° poor Ophelia
Divided from herself and her fair judgment,   85
Without the which we are pictures° or mere beasts;
Last, and as much containing as all these,°
Her brother is in secret come from France;
Feeds on his wonder, keeps himself in clouds,°
And wants not buzzers to infect his ear   90
With pestilent speeches of his father's death,
Wherein necessity, of matter beggared,
Will nothing stick our person to arraign
In ear and ear.° O my dear Gertrude, this,
Like to a murd'ring piece, in many places   95
Gives me superfluous death.°

A noise within.

Queen.   Alack, what noise is this?
King.
    Where are my Switzers?° Let them guard the door.

Enter MESSENGER.

    What is the matter?

---

78.   **spies:** scouts.
80.   **author:** cause.
81.   **muddied:** muddled.
83–84. **we ... him:** We have shown immature judgment in our secret haste
       to bury him.
86.   **pictures:** merely outward forms without souls.
87.   **and ... these:** as much of equal importance.
89.   **in clouds:** in uncertainty.
92–94. **Wherein ... ear:** in which, ignorant of the facts, he may then accuse
       us to everyone.
95–96. **murdering-piece ... death:** loaded cannon, capable of overkill.
97.   **Switzers:** Swiss guards.

Messenger.   Save yourself, my lord:
   The ocean, overpeering of his list,
   Eats not the flats° with more impetuous haste   100
   Than young Laertes, in a riotous head,°
   O'erbears your officers. The rabble call him lord;
   And, as the world were now but to begin,
   Antiquity forgot, custom not known,
   The ratifiers and props of every word,°   105
   They cry "Choose we, Laertes shall be king!"
   Caps, hands, and tongues applaud it to the clouds,
   "Laertes shall be king! Laertes king!"°

A noise within.

Queen.
   How cheerfully on the false trail they cry!°
   O, this is counter,° you false Danish dogs!   110
King.
   The doors are broke.

Enter LAERTES *with* DANES.

Laertes.
   Where is this king? —Sirs, stand you all without.
Danes.
   No, let's come in!
Laertes.   I pray you give me leave.
Danes.
   We will, we will!

                    Exeunt DANES.

99–100. **overpeering … flats:** overflowing its boundary, does not flood the
    flatlands.
101.   **in … head:** heading a force of others.
104–05. **Antiquity … word:** forgetting ancient rules and customs, which
    are the basis of any motto.
108.   **Laertes … king:** Denmark was an elective monarchy.
109.   **cry:** bay (like hounds following a scent).
110.   **counter:** the wrong direction (a hunting term).

Laertes.

I thank you. Keep the door.

O thou vile king,   115

Give me my father!

Queen.   Calmly, good Laertes.

Laertes.

That drop of blood that's calm proclaims me bastard;

Cries cuckold° to my father; brands° the harlot

Even here, between the chaste unsmirched brows

Of my true mother.

King.   What is the cause, Laertes,   120

That thy rebellion looks so giantlike?

Let him go, Gertrude. Do not fear° our person.

There's such divinity doth hedge° a king

That treason can but peep° to what it would,

Acts little of his° will. Tell me, Laertes,   125

Why thou art thus incensed. Let him go, Gertrude.

Speak, man.

Laertes.

Where is my father?

King.   Dead.

Queen.   But not by him!

King.

Let him demand his fill.°

Laertes.

How came he dead? I'll not be juggled with: 130

To hell, allegiance! vows, to the blackest devil!

Conscience and grace,° to the profoundest pit!

I dare damnation. To this point I stand,

---

118. **cuckold:** a deceived husband. **brands:** Convicted harlots were
    branded on the forehead. (See Act III, Scene 4, lines 43–45.)
122. **fear:** fear for.
123. **hedge:** put a protective hedge around.
124. **peep:** look from a distance.
125. **his:** its.
129. **demand his fill:** ask until he is satisfied.
132. **grace:** God's grace, which leads to salvation.

That both the worlds I give to negligence,°
Let come what comes; only I'll be revenged   135
Most thoroughly for my father.

King.   Who shall stay° you?

Laertes.

My will, not all the world!°
And for my means, I'll husband them° so well
They shall go far with little.

King.   Good Laertes,
If you desire to know the certainty   140
Of your dear father's death, is't writ in your revenge
That swoopstake° you will draw both friend and foe,
Winner and loser?

Laertes.

None but his enemies.

King.   Will you know them then?

Laertes.

To his good friends thus wide I'll ope my arms   145
And like the kind life-rend'ring pelican,°
Repast them with my blood.

King.   Why, now you speak
Like a good child and a true gentleman.
That I am guiltless of your father's death,
And am most sensible° in grief for it,   150
It shall as level° to your judgment pierce
As day does to your eye.

A noise within [voices]:   "Let her come in."

---

134. **That … negligence:** I don't care what becomes of me in this world
      or the next.
136. **stay:** prevent.
137. **not … world:** nothing will stop me.
138. **husband them:** use them economically.
142. **swoopstake:** indiscriminately.
146. **pelican:** According to popular belief, the pelican pecked at its breast
      to feed its blood to its young.
150. **sensible:** feelingly.
151. **level:** directly.

Laertes.
How now! what noise is that?

Enter OPHELIA.

O heat, dry up my brains! Tears seven times salt
Burn out the sense and virtue° of mine eye!   155
By heaven, thy madness shall be paid by weight
Till our scale turn the beam.° O rose of May!°
Dear maid, kind sister, sweet Ophelia!
O heavens! is't possible a young maid's wits
Should be as mortal as an old man's life?   160
Nature is fine in love, and where 'tis fine,
It sends some precious instance of itself
After the thing it loves.°

Ophelia. [*Sings.*]
> They bore him barefaced on the bier
>   Hey non nony, nony, hey nony   165
> And in his grave rained many a tear.

Fare you well, my dove!

Laertes.
Hadst thou thy wits, and didst persuade revenge,
It could not move thus.

Ophelia. You must sing "A-down, a-down," and you,   170
"Call him a-down-a." O, how the wheel° becomes
it! It is the false steward, that stole his master's
daughter.°

Laertes. This nothing's more than matter.°

---

155. **virtue:** power.
157. **Till ... beam:** until the scale tips in our favor. **rose of May:** perfection
    of youthful beauty.
161–63. **Nature ... loves:** It is human nature to love, and Ophelia's love (for
    Polonius and Hamlet) was so noble that she gave her sanity as a
    token of it.
171. **wheel:** refrain of her song.
172–73. **false ... daughter:** a reference to a story that is now lost.
174. **This ... matter:** This nonsense says more than sense could say.

Ophelia. There's rosemary, that's for remembrance.   175
  Pray you love, remember. And there is pansies,
  that's for thoughts.
Laertes. A document in madness! Thoughts and
  remembrance fitted.
Ophelia. There's fennel for you, and columbines.   180
  There's rue for you, and here's some for me.° We
  may call it herb of grace o' Sundays. O, you must
  wear your rue with a difference! There's a daisy.
  I would give you some violets, but they withered
  all when my father died. They say he made a   185
  good end. [*Sings.*]
      For bonny sweet Robin is all my joy.
Laertes.
  Thought and affliction, passion,° hell itself,
  She turns to favor° and to prettiness.
Ophelia. [*Sings.*]
      And will he not come again?   190
      And will he not come again?
          No, no, he is dead;
          Go to thy deathbed;
      He never will come again.

      His beard was as white as snow,   195
      All flaxen was his poll.°
          He is gone, he is gone,
          And we cast away moan.
      God 'a' mercy on his soul!
  And of° all Christian souls, I pray God. God be wi' ye. 200

                                        Exit.

175–77, 180–81. Ophelia gives rosemary and pansies to Laertes; fennel and
    columbine (for infidelity) to Gertrude; rue (for repentance) to Claudius
    and herself.
188. **passion:** suffering.
189. **favor:** charm.
196. **All ... poll:** the top of his head (his hair) was white.
200. **of:** on.

Laertes.

Do you see this, O God?

King.

Laertes, I must commune with° your grief,
Or you deny me right. Go but apart,
Make choice of whom your wisest friends you will,
And they shall hear and judge 'twixt you and me.   205
If by direct or by collateral° hand
They find us° touched,° we will our kingdom give,
Our crown, our life, and all that we call ours,
To you in satisfaction; but if not,
Be you content to lend your patience to us,   210
And we shall jointly labor with your soul
To give it due content.

Laertes.   Let this be so.

His means of death, his obscure funeral—
No trophy, sword, nor hatchment° o'er his bones,
No noble rite nor formal ostentation—   215
Cry to be heard, as 'twere from heaven to earth,
That I must call't in question.

King.   So you shall;

And where the offense is let the great axe fall.
I pray you go with me.

                                        Exeunt.

---

202. **commune with:** share.
206. **collateral:** indirect.
207. **us:** Claudius has shifted from *I* to the royal *we*. **touched:** implicated.
214. **hatchment:** coat of arms. (Polonius was dishonored by being buried
      secretly. Traditionally when a knight was buried, his sword, helmet,
      and coat of arms were hung above his tomb.)

Scene 6. *Another room in the castle.*

Enter HORATIO *and a* SERVANT.

Horatio. What are they that would speak with me?
Servant. Sailors, sir; they say they have letters
    for you.
Horatio. Let them come in.

                                           Exit SERVANT.

    I do not know from what part of the world   5
    I should be greeted, if not from Lord Hamlet.

Enter SAILORS.

First Sailor. God bless you, sir.
Horatio. Let him bless thee too.
First Sailor. He shall, sir, an't° please him. There's
    a letter for you, sir—it comes from the ambassador   10
    that was bound for England—if your name be
    Horatio, as I am let to know it is.
Horatio. [*Reads.*] *Horatio, when thou shalt have*
    overlooked° this, give these fellows some means°
    to the King. They have letters for him. Ere we   15
    were two days old at sea, a pirate of very warlike
    appointment° gave us chase. Finding ourselves
    too slow of sail, we put on a compelled valor, and
    in the grapple I boarded them. On the instant
    they got clear of our ship; so I alone became their   20
    prisoner. They have dealt with me like thieves
    of mercy;° but they knew what they did: I am to
    do a good turn for them. Let the King have the
    letters I have sent; and repair thou to me with as
    much speed as thou wouldst fly death. I have   25

IV.6.9. an't: if it.
14.   **overlooked:** read. **means:** access.
17.   **appointment:** equipment.
21–22. thieves of mercy: merciful thieves. (The phrase is an ironic echo of
    "angels of mercy.")

words to speak in thine ear will make thee dumb;
yet are they much too light for the bore of the
matter.° These good fellows will bring thee where
I am. Rosencrantz and Guildenstern hold their
course for England. Of them I have much to tell   30
thee. Farewell.

         He that thou knowest thine, HAMLET.

Come, I will give you way° for these your letters,
And do't the speedier that you may direct me
To him from whom you brought them.   35

                         Exeunt.

Scene 7. *Another room in the castle.*

Enter KING CLAUDIUS *and* LAERTES.

King.
     Now must your conscience my acquittance seal,°
     And you must put me in your heart for friend,
     Sith you have heard, and with a knowing° ear,
     That he which hath your noble father slain
     Pursued my life.
Laertes.   It well appears. But tell me   5
     Why you proceeded not against these feats°
     So crimeful and so capital° in nature,
     As by your safety, wisdom, all things else,
     You mainly were stirred up.
King.   O, for two special reasons,
     Which may to you, perhaps, seem much unsinewed,°   10

27–28. **are … matter:** are overshadowed by the enormity of the situation.
       (The metaphor is that of a cannon with a bore too large for the shot,
       which will then fall short of the mark.)
33.   **way:** means of success (see line 14).
IV.7.1. **my … seal:** acquit me.
3.   **knowing:** knowledgeable.
6.   **feats:** wicked acts.
7.   **capital:** punishable by death.
10.   **much unsinewed:** very feeble.

But yet to me they are strong. The Queen his mother
Lives almost by his looks; and for myself—
My virtue or my plague, be it either which°—
She's so conjunctive to my life and soul
That, as the star moves not but in his sphere,°   15
I could not but by her. The other motive
Why to a public count I might not go
Is the great love the general gender bear him,
Who, dipping all his faults in their affection,
Would, like the spring that turneth wood to stone,°   20
Convert his gyves to graces;° so that my arrows,
Too slightly timbered° for so loud a wind,
Would have reverted to my bow again,
And not where I had aimed them.

Laertes.

And so have I a noble father lost;   25
A sister driven into desp'rate terms,°
Whose worth, if praises may go back again,°
Stood challenger on mount of all the age
For her perfections.° But my revenge will come.

King.

Break not your sleeps for that. You must not think   30
That we are made of stuff so flat and dull
That we can let our beard be shook with danger,
And think it pastime. You shortly shall hear more.°
I loved your father, and we love ourself,
And that, I hope, will teach you to imagine—   35

---

13.   **be ... which:** whichever it is.
15.   **not ... sphere:** only in its own sphere.
20.   **spring ... stone:** a reference to springs with heavy mineral content that can petrify wood.
21.   **Convert ... graces:** regard his chains as adornments.
22.   **Too ... timbered:** with a shaft too light in weight.
26.   **terms:** condition.
27.   **if ... again:** if one may praise her for the way she was formerly.
28–29. **Stood ... perfections:** challenged the world to find her equal.
33.   **You ... more:** a reference to what the king hopes to hear from England. The irony is made clear a few lines later.

Enter a MESSENGER *with letters.*

How now! What news?

Messenger.   Letters, my lord, from Hamlet:
This to your Majesty; this to the Queen.

King.
From Hamlet! Who brought them?

Messenger.
Sailors, my lord, they say; I saw them not.
They were given me by Claudio; he received them   40
Of him that brought them.

King.   Laertes, you shall hear them.
[*To* MESSENGER] Leave us.

                                        Exit MESSENGER.

[*Reads.*] *High and Mighty—You shall know I am*
set naked° on your kingdom. Tomorrow shall I
beg leave to see your kingly eyes;° when I shall   45
(first asking your pardon thereunto) recount the
occasion of my sudden and more strange return.
                                        HAMLET.
What should this mean? Are all the rest come back?
Or is it some abuse,° and no such thing?   50

Laertes.
Know you the hand?

King.   'Tis Hamlet's character.°
"Naked!"
And in a postscript here, he says "alone."
Can you advise me?

Laertes.
I'm lost in it, my lord. But let him come!

---

44.   **naked:** lacking all.
45.   **your ... eyes:** you in person.
50.   **abuse:** deception.
51.   **character:** handwriting.

It warms the very sickness in my heart   55
That I shall live and tell him to his teeth,
"Thus didest° thou."
King.   If it be so, Laertes
(As how should it be so? how otherwise?),
Will you be ruled by me?
Laertes.   Ay, my lord,
So you will not o'errule° me to a peace.   60
King.
To thine own peace. If he be now returned,
As checking at° his voyage, and that he means
No more to undertake it, I will work him
To an exploit now ripe in my device,
Under the which he shall not choose but fall;   65
And for his death no wind of blame shall breathe,
But even his mother shall uncharge the practice°
And call it accident.
Laertes.   My lord, I will be ruled;
The rather, if you could devise it so
That I might be the organ.°
King.   It falls right.°   70
You have been talked of since your travel much,
And that in Hamlet's hearing, for a quality
Wherein they say you shine. Your sum of parts°
Did not together pluck such envy from him
As did that one; and that, in my regard,   75
Of the unworthiest siege.°
Laertes.   What part is that, my lord?

---

57.   **didest:** Some versions have *diest* instead of *didest*.
60.   **o'errule:** command.
62.   **checking at:** shying from, stopping in mid-course.
67.   **uncharge the practice:** not suspect the ruse.
70.   **organ:** means. **falls right:** fits in with the plan.
73.   **sum of parts:** total abilities.
76.   **siege:** place (or rank).

King.
A very riband° in the cap of youth—
Yet needful too; for youth no less becomes
The light and careless livery° that it wears
Than settled age his sables and his weeds,°   80
Importing health and graveness.° Two months since
Here was a gentleman of Normandy.
I have seen myself, and served against, the French,
And they can well° on horseback; but this gallant
Had witchcraft in't. He grew unto his seat,   85
And to such wondrous doing brought his horse,
As he had been incorpsed and demi-natured°
With the brave beast. So far he topped my thought°
That I, in forgery of shapes and tricks,°
Come short of what he did.
Laertes.   A Norman was't?   90
King. A Norman.
Laertes.
Upon my life, Lamound.
King.   The very same.
Laertes.
I know him well. He is the brooch° indeed
And gem of all the nation.
King.
He made confession of you;°   95
And gave you such a masterly report
For art and exercise in your defense,°

---

77.   **very riband:** mere decoration.
79.   **livery:** outfit.
80.   **sables ... weeds:** somber garments.
81.   **Importing ... graveness:** signifying stability and seriousness.
84.   **can well:** are highly skilled.
87.   **As ... demi-natured:** as if he had grown into one body.
88.   **topped my thought:** did more than I could imagine.
89.   **in ... tricks:** in inventing feats of skill.
93.   **brooch:** ornament.
95.   **made ... you:** attested that he knew you.
97.   **defense:** swordsmanship.

And for your rapier most especially,
That he cried out 'twould be a sight indeed
If one could match you. The scrimers° of their nation   100
He swore had had neither motion, guard, nor eye,
If you opposed them. Sir, this report of his
Did Hamlet so envenom with his envy
That he could nothing do but wish and beg
Your sudden coming o'er to play with him.   105
Now, out of this—

Laertes.   What out of this, my lord?

King.

Laertes, was your father dear to you?
Or are you like the painting of a sorrow,
A face without a heart?

Laertes.   Why ask you this?

King.

Not that I think you did not love your father;   110
But that I know love is begun by time,
And that I see, in passages of proof,°
Time qualifies° the spark and fire of it.
There lives within the very flame of love
A kind of wick or snuff that will abate it;   115
And nothing is at a like goodness still;°
For goodness, growing to a plurisy,°
Dies in his° own too-much. That we would do,
We should do when we would;° for this "would"
    changes,
And hath abatements and delays as many   120
As there are tongues, are hands, are accidents;
And then this "should" is like a spendthrift sigh,

---

100. **scrimers:** fencers.
112. **in ... proof:** in instances that prove it.
113. **qualifies:** lessens.
116. **still:** always.
117. **plurisy:** excess.
118. **his:** its.
119. **We ... would:** we should act when we have the will.

That hurts by easing.° But to the quick o' the ulcer!°
Hamlet comes back. What would you undertake
To show yourself your father's son in deed   125
More than in words?
Laertes.   To cut his throat i' the church!
King.
No place indeed should murder sanctuarize;°
Revenge should have no bounds. But, good Laertes,
Will you do this? Keep close within your chamber.
Hamlet returned shall know you are come home.   130
We'll put on those° shall praise your excellence
And set a double varnish on the fame
The Frenchman gave you; bring you in fine° together
And wager on your heads. He, being remiss,°
Most generous,° and free from all contriving,   135
Will not peruse° the foils; so that with ease,
Or with a little shuffling, you may choose
A sword unbated,° and, in a pass of practice,°
Requite him for your father.
Laertes.   I will do't!
And, for that purpose I'll anoint my sword.   140
I bought an unction of a mountebank,°
So mortal that, but dip a knife in it,
Where it draws blood no cataplasm° so rare,
Collected from all simples° that have virtue

122–23. **this … easing:** our obligations, when acted on, ease our conscience but harm us by weakening our moral perception.
123. **quick … ulcer:** heart of the trouble.
127. **sanctuarize:** give sanctuary to.
131. **put on those:** incite those who.
133. **in fine:** finally.
134. **remiss:** careless.
135. **generous:** magnanimous.
136. **peruse:** look carefully at.
138. **unbated:** not blunted. (Rapiers used in a fencing match would have blunt tips.) **pass of practice:** treacherous thrust.
141. **mountebank:** quack.
143. **cataplasm:** poultice.
144. **simples:** herbs.

Under the moon,° can save the thing from death   145
That is but scratched withal. I'll touch my point
With this contagion, that, if I gall° him slightly,
It may be death.
King.   Let's further think of this,
Weigh what convenience both of time and means
May fit us to our shape.° If this should fail,   150
And that our drift look through our bad performance,°
'Twere better not assayed. Therefore this project
Should have a back or second, that might hold
If this should blast in proof.° Soft! let me see.
We'll make a solemn wager on your cunnings°—   155
I ha't!°
When in your motion you are hot and dry—
As make your bouts more violent to that end—
And that he calls for drink, I'll have prepared him
A chalice for the nonce;° whereon but sipping,   160
If he by chance escape your venomed stuck,°
Our purpose may hold there. —But stay, what noise?

Enter QUEEN GERTRUDE.

How now, sweet queen?
Queen.
One woe doth tread upon another's heel,
So fast they follow. Your sister's drowned, Laertes.   165

---

145. **Under the moon:** Herbs collected in moonlight were thought to be highly powerful.
147. **gall:** graze.
150. **fit ... shape:** suit our plan.
151. **our drift ... performance:** Our intention is revealed through inept performance.
154. **blast in proof:** come apart when tried out.
155. **cunnings:** skill.
156. **ha't:** have it.
160. **nonce:** occasion.
161. **stuck:** sword thrust.

Laertes. Drowned! O, where?

Queen.

> There is a willow grows aslant° a brook,
> That shows his hoar° leaves in the glassy stream.
> There with fantastic garlands did she come
> Of crowflowers, nettles, daisies, and long purples,°   170
> That liberal° shepherds give a grosser name,
> But our cold maids do dead men's fingers call them.
> There, on the pendent° boughs her coronet weeds°
> Clamb'ring to hang, an envious sliver° broke;
> When down her weedy trophies and herself   175
> Fell in the weeping brook. Her clothes spread wide
> And, mermaid-like, awhile they bore her up;
> Which time she chanted snatches of old tunes,
> As one incapable of° her own distress,
> Or like a creature native and indued   180
> Unto° that element; but long it could not be
> Till that her garments, heavy with their drink,
> Pulled the poor wretch from her melodious lay°
> To muddy death.

Laertes.   Alas, then, she is drowned?

Queen. Drowned, drowned.   185

Laertes.

> Too much of water hast thou, poor Ophelia,
> And therefore I forbid my tears; but yet
> It is our trick;° nature her custom holds,
> Let shame say what it will. When these are gone,

---

167. **aslant:** slanting above.
168. **his hoar:** its gray.
170. **long purples:** kind of orchid.
171. **liberal:** loose-talking.
173. **pendent:** drooping. **coronet weeds:** flowers woven into a crown.
174. **envious sliver:** malicious branch.
179. **incapable of:** not realizing.
180–81. **indued Unto:** adapted to live in.
183. **lay:** song.
188. **our trick:** human nature (to cry).

The woman will be out.° Adieu, my lord.   190
I have a speech of fire, that fain would blaze
But that this folly douts° it.

Exit.

King.   Let's follow, Gertrude.
How much I had to do to calm his rage!
Now fear I this will give it start again;
Therefore let's follow.   195

Exeunt.

---

190.   The ... out: My female traits (crying) will be done with.
192.   douts: extinguishes.

Act V

Scene 1. *A churchyard.*

Enter two CLOWNS, *with spades and pickaxes.*

First Clown. Is she to be buried in Christian burial that
willfully seeks her own salvation?°
Second Clown. I tell thee she is; and therefore make
her grave straight.° The crowner° hath sat on her,
and finds it Christian burial.   5
First Clown. How can that be, unless she drowned
herself in her own defense?
Second Clown. Why, 'tis found so.
First Clown. It must be se offendendo;° it cannot be
else. For here lies the point: if I drown myself   10
wittingly, it argues an act; and an act hath three
branches—it is, to act, to do, to perform; argal,°
she drowned herself wittingly.
Second Clown. Nay, but hear you, Goodman Delver!°
First Clown. Give me leave.° Here lies the water;   15
good. Here stands the man; good. If the man go to
this water and drown himself, it is, will he nill he,°
he goes—mark you that. But if the water come to
him and drown him, he drowns not himself. Argal,
he that is not guilty of his own death shortens not   20
his own life.
Second Clown. But is this law?

V.1.1–2. Christian ... salvation: Christian burial was denied to suicides.
4.   **straight:** immediately. **crowner:** coroner. (The coroner had found
          Ophelia's death accidental.)
9.   **se offendendo:** The clown confuses self-offense (*se offendendo*) with
          self-defense.
12.   **argal:** a mispronunciation of *ergo,* Latin for "therefore."
14.   **Delver:** digger.
15.   **Give me leave:** Let me continue.
17.   **will he, nill he:** whether he wants to or not.

First Clown. Ay, marry, is't—crowner's quest° law.
Second Clown. Will you ha' the truth on't? If this
    had not been a gentlewoman, she should have   25
    been buried out o' Christian burial.
First Clown. Why, there thou say'st! And the more
    pity that great folk should have count'nance° in
    this world to drown or hang themselves, more
    than their even-Christian.° Come, my spade!   30
    There is no ancient gentleman but gard'ners,°
    ditchers, and grave-makers. They hold up°
    Adam's profession.
Second Clown. Was he a gentleman?
First Clown. He was the first that ever bore arms.°   35
Second Clown. Why, he had none.
First Clown. What, art a heathen? How dost thou
    understand the Scripture? The Scripture says
    Adam digged. Could he dig without arms? I'll
    put another question to thee. If thou answerest   40
    me not to the purpose, confess thyself°—
Second Clown. Go to!°
First Clown. What is he that builds stronger than
    either the mason, the shipwright, or the carpenter?
Second Clown. The gallows-maker; for that frame   45
    outlives a thousand tenants.
First Clown. I like thy wit well, in good faith. The
    gallows does well. But how does it well? It does

---

23.   **quest:** inquest.
28.   **count'nance:** favor.
30.   **even-Christian:** fellow Christians.
31.   **no ... gard'ners:** no gentlemen in olden days except gardeners. (The
        clowns have misunderstood the famous verse "When Adam delved
        and Eve span [spun], who was then the gentleman?")
32.   **hold up:** keep up.
35.   **first ... arms:** the first to have a coat of arms (a sign of a gentleman).
41.   **confess thyself:** The entire expression is "confess thyself and be
        hanged."
42.   **Go to:** Get on with you!

well to those that do ill. Now, thou dost ill to say
the gallows is built stronger than the church.   50
Argal, the gallows may do well to thee. To't
again, come.
Second Clown. Who builds stronger than a mason, a
shipwright, or a carpenter?
First Clown. Ay, tell me that, and unyoke.°   55
Second Clown. Marry, now I can tell.
First Clown. To't.
Second Clown. Mass, I cannot tell.

Enter HAMLET *and* HORATIO, *at a distance.*

First Clown. Cudgel thy brains no more about it, for
your dull ass will not mend his pace with beating;   60
and when you are asked this question next, say
"a grave-maker." The houses he makes last
till doomsday. Go, get thee to Yaughan;° fetch me
a stoup° of liquor.

                                    Exit SECOND CLOWN.
[FIRST CLOWN *digs and sings.*]

    In youth, when I did love, did love,   65
      Methought it was very sweet;
    To contract°—O—the time, for—a—my behove,°
      O, methought, there—a—was nothing—
      a—meet.

Hamlet. Has this fellow no feeling of his business,
that he sings at grave-making?   70
Horatio. Custom hath made it in him a property of
easiness.°

---

55.   **unyoke:** finish the job. (A day's work ended with unyoking the oxen.)
63.   **Yaughan:** probably the name of a London innkeeper.
64.   **stoup:** large cup.
67.   **contract:** shorten. **behove:** benefit.
71–72. **Custom … easiness:** He has become accustomed to it and gives it no thought.

Hamlet. 'Tis e'en so. The hand of little employment
hath the daintier sense.°
First Clown. [*Sings.*]

> But age with his stealing steps   75
>   Hath clawed me in his clutch,
> And hath shipped me intil the land,
>   As if I had never been such.

[*Throws up a skull.*]

Hamlet. That skull had a tongue in it, and could sing
once. How the knave jowls° it to the ground, as if   80
'twere Cain's jawbone, that did the first murder!
It might be the pate of a politician,° which this
ass now o'erreaches;° one that would circumvent
God, might it not?
Horatio. It might, my lord.   85
Hamlet. Or of a courtier, which could say "Good
morrow, sweet lord! How dost thou, good lord?"
This might be my Lord Such-a-one, that praised
my Lord Such-a-one's horse when he meant to beg
it—might it not?   90
Horatio. Ay, my lord.
Hamlet. Why, e'en so! and now my Lady Worm's,
chapless,° and knocked about the mazzard° with a
sexton's spade. Here's fine revolution,° if we had
the trick° to see't. Did these bones cost no more the   95
breeding, but to play at loggats° with 'em? Mine
ache to think on't.

73–74. The hand ... sense: Those with little to do have more delicate
     feelings.
80.   jowls: knocks.
82.   politician: schemer.
83.   o'erreaches: has an advantage over.
93.   chapless: without a lower jaw. **mazzard:** slang for "head."
94.   revolution: a turning around.
95.   trick: knack.
96.   loggats: a game played by tossing wooden pieces at a stake in the
     ground.

First Clown. [*Sings.*]
> *A pick-axe and a spade, a spade,*
> > *For and° a shrouding sheet;*
> *O, a pit of clay for to be made*   100
> > *For such a guest is meet.*

[*Throws up another skull.*]

Hamlet. There's another. Why may not that be the
skull of a lawyer? Where be his quiddities now,
his quillets,° his cases, his tenures,° and his tricks?
Why does he suffer this rude knave now to knock   105
him about the sconce° with a dirty shovel, and
will not tell him of his action of battery? Hum!
This fellow might be in's time a great buyer of land,
with his statutes, his recognizances, his fines, his
double vouchers, his recoveries.° Is this the fine°   110
of his fines, and the recovery of his recoveries, to
have his fine pate full of fine dirt? Will his
vouchers vouch° him no more of his purchases, and
double ones too, than the length and breadth of a
pair of indentures?° The very conveyances° of his   115
lands will scarcely lie in this box;° and must the
inheritor° himself have no more, ha?

Horatio. Not a jot more, my lord.

Hamlet. Is not parchment made of sheepskins?

Horatio. Ay, my lord, and of calveskins too.   120

---

99. **For and:** and also his.
103–04. **quiddities ... quillets:** his quibbling arguments now.
104. **tenures:** titles to property.
106. **sconce:** head.
109–10. **statutes ... recoveries:** legal terms used in the sale of property.
110. **fine:** final result.
113. **vouch:** guarantee.
115. **indentures:** contracts. **conveyances:** deeds.
116. **box:** deed box (and coffin).
117. **inheritor:** acquirer.

Hamlet. They are sheep and calves which seek out
   assurance in that. I will speak to this fellow.
   Whose grave's this, sirrah?

First Clown. Mine, sir. [*Sings.*]
        O, a pit of clay for to be made   125
            For such a guest is meet.

Hamlet. I think it be thine indeed, for thou liest in't.

First Clown. You lie out on't, sir, and therefore 'tis
   not yours. For my part, I do not lie in't, yet it is
   mine.   130

Hamlet. Thou dost lie in't, to be in't and say it is
   thine. 'Tis for the dead, not for the quick;°
   therefore thou liest.

First Clown. 'Tis a quick lie, sir; 'twill away again
   from me to you.   135

Hamlet. What man dost thou dig it for?

First Clown. For no man, sir.

Hamlet. What woman, then?

First Clown. For none neither.

Hamlet. Who is to be buried in't?   140

First Clown. One that was a woman, sir; but, rest her
   soul, she's dead.

Hamlet. How absolute° the knave is! We must speak
   by the card,° or equivocation° will undo us. By the
   Lord, Horatio, this three years I have taken   145
   note of it, the age is grown so picked that the toe
   of the peasant comes so near the heel of the courtier
   he galls his kibe.° — How long hast thou been a
   grave-maker?

---

132. **quick:** living.
143. **absolute:** precise.
144. **by the card:** accurately. **equivocation:** speaking in double meanings.
146–48. **so … kibe:** so refined that the peasant is not far behind the
      courtier's heels.

First Clown. Of all the days i' the year, I came to't   150
    that day that our last king Hamlet overcame
    Fortinbras.

Hamlet. How long is that since?

First Clown. Cannot you tell that? Every fool can tell
    that. It was the very day that young Hamlet was   155
    born—he that is mad, and sent into England.

Hamlet. Ay, marry, why was he sent into England?

First Clown. Why, because he was mad. He shall
    recover his wits there; or, if he do not, 'tis no great
    matter there.   160

Hamlet. Why?

First Clown. 'Twill not be seen in him there. There
    the men are as mad as he.

Hamlet. How came he mad?

First Clown. Very strangely, they say.   165

Hamlet. How strangely?

First Clown. Faith, e'en with losing his wits.

Hamlet. Upon what ground?

First Clown. Why, here in Denmark. I have been
    sexton here, man and boy, thirty years.   170

Hamlet. How long will a man lie i' the earth ere he
    rot?

First Clown. Faith, if he be not rotten before he die
    (as we have many pocky° corses now-a-days that
    will scarce hold° the laying in), he will last you   175
    some eight year or nine year. A tanner will last
    you nine year.

Hamlet. Why he more than another?

First Clown. Why, sir, his hide is so tanned with
    his trade that he will keep out water a great   180
    while; and your water is a sore° decayer of your

---

174. **pocky:** pox-ridden.
175. **hold:** endure.
181. **sore:** intense.

whoreson° dead body. Here's a skull now: this
skull has lien you i' th' earth three-and-twenty years.
Hamlet. Whose was it?
First Clown. A whoreson mad fellow's it was. Whose   185
do you think it was?
Hamlet. Nay, I know not.
First Clown. A pestilence on him for a mad rogue! He
poured a flagon of Rhenish on my head once. This
same skull, sir, was Yorick's skull, the King's   190
jester.
Hamlet. This?
First Clown. E'en that.
Hamlet. Let me see. [*Takes the skull.*] Alas, poor
Yorick! I knew him, Horatio. A fellow of infinite   195
jest, of most excellent fancy. He hath borne me on
his back a thousand times. And now, how abhorred
in my imagination it is! My gorge rises° at it. Here
hung those lips that I have kissed I know not how
oft. Where be your gibes° now? your gambols?   200
your songs? your flashes of merriment that were
wont to set the table on a roar? Not one now, to
mock your own grinning? Quite chapfall'n?° Now
get you to my lady's chamber, and tell her, let her
paint an inch thick, to this favor she must come.   205
Make her laugh at that. Prithee, Horatio, tell me
one thing.
Horatio. What's that, my lord?
Hamlet. Dost thou think Alexander° looked o' this
fashion i' the earth?   210
Horatio. E'en so.

---

182. **whoreson:** a general term of abuse.
198. **my gorge rises:** I feel revulsion (literally, "my throat constricts").
200. **gibes:** taunts.
203. **chap-fall'n:** down-in-the-mouth (both literally and figuratively).
209. **Alexander:** Alexander the Great (356–323 B.C.).

Hamlet. And smelt so? Pah!

Puts down the skull.

Horatio. E'en so, my lord.

Hamlet. To what base uses we may return, Horatio!
Why may not imagination trace the noble dust of   215
Alexander till he find it stopping a bunghole?°

Horatio. 'Twere to consider too curiously,° to
consider so.

Hamlet. No, faith, not a jot; but to follow him thither
with modesty° enough, and likelihood to lead it;   220
as thus: Alexander died, Alexander was buried,
Alexander returneth into dust; the dust is earth;
of earth we make loam; and why of that loam
(whereto he was converted) might they not stop
a beer barrel?   225
    Imperious° Caesar, dead and turned to clay,
    Might stop a hole to keep the wind away.
    O, that earth which kept the world in awe
    Should patch a wall t' expel the winter flaw!°
But soft! but soft! aside! Here comes the King—   230

Enter PRIEST *and* LORDS *in procession; the corpse of* OPHELIA,
LAERTES, *and* MOURNERS *following;* KING CLAUDIUS, QUEEN
GERTRUDE, *their* ATTENDANTS.

    The Queen, the courtiers. Who is this they follow?
    And with such maimed° rites? This doth betoken
    The corse they follow did with desp'rate hand
    Fordo its° own life. 'Twas of some estate.°
    Couch we° awhile, and mark.   235

---

216. **bunghole:** hole in a barrel (see line 225).
217. **curiously:** ingeniously.
220. **modesty:** moderation.
226. **Imperious:** imperial.
229. **flaw:** gust of wind.
232. **maimed:** incomplete. (The *ed* is pronounced as a separate syllable.)
234. **Fordo its:** destroy its. **estate:** high rank.
235. **Couch we:** Let us hide ourselves.

Retires with HORATIO.

Laertes.
What ceremony else?
Hamlet.   That is Laertes,
A very noble youth. Mark.
Laertes.
What ceremony else?
Priest.
Her obsequies have been as far enlarged
As we have warranty.° Her death was doubtful;°   240
And, but that great command o'ersways the order,°
She should in ground unsanctified have lodged
Till the last trumpet.° For° charitable prayers,
Shards, flints, and pebbles should be thrown on her.
Yet here she is allowed her virgin crants,°   245
Her maiden strewments,° and the bringing home
Of bell and burial.°
Laertes.
Must there no more be done?
Priest.   No more be done.
We should profane the service of the dead
To sing a requiem and such rest to her   250
As to peace-parted souls.°
Laertes.   Lay her i' the earth,
And from her fair and unpolluted flesh
May violets spring! I tell thee, churlish priest,
A minist'ring angel shall my sister be

239–40. **Her ... warranty:** Her funeral rites are as complete as are allowed.
240. **doubtful:** suspicious.
241. **but ... order:** except that the king overruled the practice.
243. **last trumpet:** Judgment Day. **For:** instead of.
245. **crants:** garland. (From the German *Kranz; Rosencrantz* means "rose garland" or "rosary.")
246. **maiden strewments:** flowers strewn on a maiden's grave.
246–47. **the ... burial:** the church bell and burial rites bringing her to her final resting place.
249–51. **We ... souls:** Canon law forbade Masses for suicides.

When thou liest howling.°

Hamlet.   What, the fair Ophelia!   255
Queen.
    Sweets to the sweet! Farewell!

Scatters flowers.

    I hoped thou shouldst have been my Hamlet's wife;
    I thought thy bride-bed to have decked,° sweet maid,
    And not have strewed thy grave.
Laertes.   O, treble woe
    Fall ten times treble on that cursed head   260
    Whose wicked deed thy most ingenious sense°
    Deprived thee of! Hold off the earth awhile,
    Till I have caught her once more in mine arms.

Leaps into the grave.

    Now pile your dust upon
        the quick and dead
    Till of this flat a mountain you have made   265
    To o'ertop old Pelion° or the skyish head
    Of blue Olympus.
Hamlet. [*Advances.*] What is he whose grief
    Bears such an emphasis? whose phrase of sorrow
    Conjures the wand'ring stars, and makes them stand°
    Like wonder-wounded hearers? This is I,   270
    Hamlet the Dane.

Leaps into the grave.

Laertes.   The devil take thy soul!

---

255. **howling:** howling in torment in Hell.
258. **thy … decked:** a reference to the custom of strewing flowers on the
      bridal bed.
261. **most … sense:** quick mind.
266. **Pelion:** In Greek legend, the giants, at war with the gods, piled
      Mount Pelion on top of Mount Ossa to reach the top of Olympus,
      home of the gods.
269. **Conjures … stand:** casts a spell on the planets and makes them
      stand still.

They grapple.

Hamlet.

    Thou pray'st not well.

    I prithee take thy fingers from my throat;

    For, though I am not splenitive° and rash,

    Yet have I something in me dangerous,   275

    Which let thy wisdom fear. Hold off thy hand!

King.

    Pluck them asunder.

Queen.   Hamlet, Hamlet!

All.

    Gentlemen!

Horatio.   Good my lord, be quiet.

The ATTENDANTS *part them, and they come out of the grave.*

Hamlet.

    Why, I will fight with him upon this theme

    Until my eyelids will no longer wag.   280

Queen.

    O my son, what theme?

Hamlet.

    I loved Ophelia. Forty thousand brothers

    Could not, with all their quantity of love,

    Make up my sum. What wilt thou do for her?

King.

    O, he is mad, Laertes.   285

Queen.

    For love of God, forbear him°!

Hamlet.

    'Swounds, show me what thou't° do.

    Woo't° weep? woo't fight? woo't fast? woo't tear

        thyself?

    Woo't drink up eisell?° eat a crocodile?

---

274. **splenitive:** hot-tempered.
286. **forbear him:** leave him alone.
287. **thou'lt:** thou wilt.
288. **Woo't:** wilt thou.
289. **eisell:** vinegar.

I'll do't. Dost thou come here to whine?   290
To outface me° with leaping in her grave?
Be buried quick° with her, and so will I.
And if thou prate of mountains, let them throw
Millions of acres on us, till our ground,°
Singeing his° pate against the burning zone,°   295
Make Ossa° like a wart! Nay, an thou'lt° mouth,
I'll rant as well as thou.
Queen.   This is mere madness;
And thus a while the fit will work on him.
Anon, as patient as the female dove
When that her golden couplets are disclosed,°   300
His silence will sit drooping.
Hamlet.   Hear you, sir!
What is the reason that you use me thus?
I loved you ever. But it is no matter.
Let Hercules° himself do what he may,
The cat will mew, and dog will have his day.   305

Exit.

King.
I pray you, good Horatio, wait upon him.

Exit HORATIO.

To LAERTES.
Strengthen your patience in° our last night's speech.
We'll put the matter to the present push. —°
Good Gertrude, set some watch over your son. —

---

291. **outface me:** get the better of me.
292. **quick:** alive.
294. **ground:** burial ground.
295. **his:** its. **burning zone:** the celestial zone in which the sun moves.
296. **Ossa:** See note for line 266. **an thou'lt:** if thou wilt.
300. **her ... disclosed:** her two yellow-downed chicks are hatched.
304. **Hercules:** Hercules is known for performing impossible tasks and for ranting.
307. **in:** in thinking about.
308. **the present push:** immediate action.

This grave shall have a living° monument.   310
An hour of quiet shortly shall we see;
Till then, in patience our proceeding be.

                                                    Exeunt.

Scene 2. *A hall in the castle.*

Enter HAMLET *and* HORATIO.

Hamlet.
So much for this, sir; now shall you see the other.
You do remember all the circumstance?
Horatio.
Remember it, my lord!
Hamlet.
Sir, in my heart there was a kind of fighting
That would not let me sleep. Methought I lay   5
Worse than the mutines in the bilboes.° Rashly—
And praised be rashness for it; let us know,°
Our indiscretion sometime serves us well,
When our deep plots do pall;° and that should learn us
There's a divinity that shapes our ends,   10
Rough-hew them how we will—
Horatio.   That is most certain.
Hamlet.
Up from my cabin,
My sea-gown scarfed° about me, in the dark
Groped I to find out them;° had my desire,
Fingered° their packet, and in fine° withdrew   15

---

310.   **living:** lasting. (This is a veiled threat to Hamlet: Claudius implies
       that one who is now living will be this grave's monument.)
V.2.6. **mutines … bilboes:** mutineers in shackles.
7.   **let us know:** note well.
9.   **pall:** fail.
13.   **sea-gown scarfed:** heavy coat wrapped around.
14.   **them:** Rosencrantz and Guildenstern.
15.   **Fingered:** stole. **in fine:** finally.

To mine own room again; making so bold,
My fears forgetting manners, to unseal
Their grand commission; where I found, Horatio—
O royal knavery!—an exact° command,
Larded° with many several sorts of reasons,   20
Importing° Denmark's health, and England's too,
With, ho! such bugs° and goblins in my life—
That, on the supervise, no leisure bated,°
No, not to stay° the grinding of the axe,
My head should be struck off.
Horatio.   Is't possible?   25
Hamlet.
Here's the commission; read it at more leisure.
But wilt thou hear me how I did proceed?
Horatio. I beseech you.
Hamlet.
Being thus benetted round with villainies,
Ere I could make a prologue to my brains,   30
They had begun the play.° I sat me down;
Devised a new commission; wrote it fair.°
I once did hold it, as our statists° do,
A baseness to write fair, and labored much
How to forget that learning; but, sir, now   35
It did me yeoman's° service. Wilt thou know
The effect° of what I wrote?
Horatio.   Ay, good my lord.

---

19.   **exact:** strict.
20.   **Larded:** embellished.
21.   **Importing:** concerning.
22.   **bugs:** bugbears (goblins that scare children).
23.   **on ... bated:** upon reading it, and with no time lost.
24.   **stay:** wait for.
30–31. Ere ... play: Before I could map out any plan, my mind instinctively
         went to work.
32.   **fair:** with good penmanship (as a clerk would write).
33.   **statists:** statesmen.
36.   **yeoman's:** faithful. (Yeomen were reliable English soldiers.)
37.   **effect:** meaning.

Hamlet.
> An earnest conjuration from the King,
> As England was his faithful tributary,
> As love between them like the palm might flourish,   40
> As peace should still her wheaten garland wear
> And stand a comma 'tween their amities,°
> And many such-like as's° of great charge,
> That, on the view and knowing of these contents,
> Without debatement° further, more or less,   45
> He should the bearers put to sudden death,
> Not shriving time allowed.

Horatio.   How was this sealed?

Hamlet.
> Why, even in that was heaven ordinant.°
> I had my father's signet in my purse,
> Which was the model of that Danish seal;   50
> Folded the writ up in the form of the other,
> Subscribed it, gave't the impression,° placed it safely,
> The changeling° never known. Now, the next day
> Was our sea fight; and what to this was sequent
> Thou know'st already.   55

Horatio.
> So Guildenstern and Rosencrantz go to't.°

Hamlet.
> Why, man, they did make love to this employment!
> They are not near my conscience; their defeat°
> Does by their own insinuation° grow.

---

42. **stand ... amities:** link their friendship.
43. **as's:** Legal clauses began with *as.* Hamlet puns on *asses* and the *charge* ("burden").
45. **debatement:** discussion.
48. **ordinant:** in charge.
52. **Subscribed ... impression:** signed it and stamped it with my seal.
53. **changeling:** switch.
56. **to't:** to their death.
58. **defeat:** destruction.
59. **own insinuation:** getting themselves involved.

'Tis dangerous when the baser nature comes   60
Between the pass° and fell° incensed points
Of mighty opposites.°
Horatio.   Why, what a king is this!
Hamlet.
Does it not, think'st thee, stand me now upon°—
He that hath killed my king, and whored my mother;
Popped in between the election° and my hopes;   65
Thrown out his angle° for my proper° life,
And with such coz'nage°—is't not perfect conscience
To quit° him with this arm? And is't not to be damned
To let this canker° of our nature come
In° further evil?   70
Horatio.
It must be shortly known to him from England
What is the issue of the business there.
Hamlet.
It will be short; the interim is mine,
And a man's life's no more than to say "one."
But I am very sorry, good Horatio,   75
That to Laertes I forgot myself;
For, by the image of my cause I see
The portraiture of his. I'll court his favors.
But sure the bravery° of his grief did put me
Into a tow'ring passion.
Horatio.   Peace! Who comes here?   80

Enter OSRIC.

---

61.   **pass:** thrust. **fell:** deadly.
62.   **opposites:** opponents.
63.   **Does ... upon:** Doesn't it seem to you that I have an obligation?
65.   **election:** Claudius did not succeed to the throne but was elected.
66.   **angle:** fishhook. **proper:** own.
67.   **coz'nage:** deception.
68.   **quit:** repay; kill.
69.   **canker:** spreading sore.
70.   **In:** into.
79.   **bravery:** showy display.

Osric. Your lordship is right welcome back to Denmark.

Hamlet. I humbly thank you, sir. [*Aside to* HORATIO.] Dost
know this waterfly?°

Horatio. [*Aside to* HAMLET.] No, my good lord.

Hamlet. [*Aside to* HORATIO.] Thy state is the more gracious;° 85
for 'tis a vice to know him. He hath much land, and
fertile. Let a beast be lord of beasts, and his crib
shall stand at the king's mess.° 'Tis a chough;° but,
as I say, spacious in the possession of dirt.

Osric. Sweet lord, if your lordship were at leisure, I 90
should impart a thing to you from his Majesty.

Hamlet. I will receive it, sir, with all diligence of
spirit. Put your bonnet to his right use,° 'tis for the
head.

Osric. I thank your lordship, it is very hot. 95

Hamlet. No, believe me, 'tis very cold; the wind is
northerly.

Osric. It is indifferent° cold, my lord, indeed.

Hamlet. But yet methinks it is very sultry and hot
for my complexion.° 100

Osric. Exceedingly, my lord; it is very sultry, as
'twere—I cannot tell how. But, my lord, his
Majesty bade me signify to you that he has laid a
great wager on your head. Sir, this is the matter—

Hamlet. I beseech you, remember. 105

Moves him to put on his hat.

Osric. Nay, good my lord; for mine ease, in good faith.

---

83. **waterfly:** showy, superficial person.
85. **gracious:** blessed.
87–88. **Let ... mess:** If a person is wealthy enough, he will be received at
    court. (A *crib* is a trough; *mess* means "dining hall.")
88. **chough:** well-to-do peasant. (Some scholars explain *chough* as a chat-
    tering bird.)
93. **Put ... use:** Put your hat back on.
98. **indifferent:** somewhat.
100. **complexion:** constitution.

Sir, here is newly come to court Laertes; believe me,
an absolute gentleman, full of most excellent
differences,° of very soft society° and great
showing. Indeed, to speak feelingly of him, he is   110
the card or calendar of gentry;° for you shall find
in him the continent of what part a gentleman
would see.°

Hamlet. Sir, his definement suffers no perdition in
you; though, I know, to divide him inventorially   115
would dizzy the arithmetic of memory, and yet
but yaw neither in respect of his quick sail.° But,
in the verity of extolment, I take him to be a soul
of great article° and his infusion° of such dearth
and rareness as, to make true diction of him, his   120
semblable is his mirror; and who else would trace
him, his umbrage, nothing more.°

Osric. Your lordship speaks most infallibly of him.

Hamlet. The concernancy,° sir? Why do we wrap
the gentleman in our more rawer breath?°   125

Osric. Sir?

Horatio. [*Aside to* HAMLET.] Is't not possible to
understand in another tongue?° You will do't, sir,
really.

Hamlet. What imports the nomination° of this   130
gentleman?

Osric. Of Laertes?

---

109. **differences:** talents that make him outstanding. **soft society:** good
    manners.
111. **card ... gentry:** perfect model of a gentleman.
112–13. **the continent ... see:** whatever any gentleman would expect to
    find.
116–17. **yet ... sail:** would go off course (be inaccurate) about him.
119. **article:** worth. **infusion:** inner being.
120–22. **his semblable ... more:** There are none like him, and his imitators
    would be only shadows.
124. **concernancy:** revelance.
124–25. **Why ... breath?:** Why use words, since they can't do him justice?
127–28. **Is't ... tongue?:** Can't you put it more simply?
130. **nomination:** mention.

Horatio. [*Aside to* HAMLET.] His purse is empty already;
all's golden words are spent.

Hamlet. Of him, sir.   135

Osric. I know you are not ignorant—

Hamlet. I would you did, sir; yet, in faith, if you did,
it would not much approve me.° Well, sir?

Osric. You are not ignorant of what excellence
Laertes is—   140

Hamlet. I dare not confess that, lest I should compare
with him in excellence; but to know a man well
were to know himself.°

Osric. I mean, sir, for his weapon; but in the
imputation° laid on him by them, in his meed   145
he's unfellowed.°

Hamlet. What's his weapon?

Osric. Rapier and dagger.

Hamlet. That's two of his weapons—but well.

Osric. The King, sir, hath wagered with him six   150
Barbary horses; against the which he has
imponed,° as I take it, six French rapiers and
poniards,° with their assigns,° as girdle, hangers,°
and so. Three of the carriages, in faith, are very
dear to fancy, very responsive to the hilts, most   155
delicate carriages, and of very liberal conceit.°

Hamlet. What call you the carriages?

Horatio. [*Aside to* HAMLET.] I knew you must be
edified by the margent° ere you had done.

Osric. The carriages,° sir, are the hangers.   160

137–38. **if … me:** If you did know, your opinion wouldn't matter.
142–43. **to know … himself:** to judge someone requires self-knowledge.
145. **imputation:** estimation.
145–46. **in … unfellowed:** he has no equal.
152. **imponed:** staked.
153. **poniards:** daggers. **assigns:** accessories. **girdle, hangers:** sword belt
     and straps.
156. **very liberal … conceit:** tastefully decorated with a delicate and
     lavish design.
159. **margent:** explanatory note.

Hamlet. The phrase would be more germane to the
matter if we could carry cannon by our sides. I
would it might be hangers till then. But on! Six
Barbary horses against six French swords, their
assigns, and three liberal-conceited carriages: 165
that's the French bet against the Danish. Why is
this all imponed, as you call it?

Osric. The King, sir, hath laid° that, in a dozen
passes° between yourself and him, he shall not
exceed you three hits; he hath laid on twelve for   170
nine, and it would come to immediate trial if your
lordship would vouchsafe the answer.°

Hamlet. How if I answer no?

Osric. I mean, my lord, the opposition of your person
in trial.   175

Hamlet. Sir, I will walk here in the hall. If it please
his Majesty, it is the breathing time of day with
me. Let the foils be brought, the gentleman
willing, and the King hold his purpose, I will win
for him if I can; if not, I will gain nothing but   180
my shame and the odd hits.

Osric. Shall I redeliver you e'en so?

Hamlet. To this effect, sir, after what flourish your
nature will.

Osric. I commend my duty to your lordship.   185

Hamlet. Yours, yours.

Exit OSRIC.

He does well to commend it himself; there are no
tongues else for's turn.°

Horatio. This lapwing runs away with the shell on

---

160. **carriages:** These are also the frameworks of cannons (which explains
lines 161–62).
168. **laid:** bet.
169. **passes:** bouts.
172. **answer:** answer the challenge.
188. **for's turn:** to do that for him.

his head.° 190

Hamlet. He did comply with° his dug before he
sucked it. Thus has he, and many more of the same
bevy that I know the drossy° age dotes on, only
got the tune of the time and outward habit of
encounter—a kind of yeasty collection, which 195
carries them through and through the most fanned
and winnowed opinions; and do but blow them to
their trial°—the bubbles are out.

Enter a LORD.

Lord. My lord, his Majesty commended him to you
by young Osric, who brings back to him, that you 200
attend him in the hall. He sends to know if your
pleasure hold to play with Laertes, or that you
will take longer time.

Hamlet. I am constant to my purposes; they follow
the King's pleasure. If his fitness speaks, mine is 205
ready;° now or whensoever, provided I be so able
as now.

Lord. The King and Queen and all are coming down.

Hamlet. In happy time.°

Lord. The Queen desires you to use some gentle 210
entertainment° to Laertes before you fall to play.

Hamlet. She well instructs me.

Exit LORD.

Horatio. You will lose this wager, my lord.

189–90. This ... head: a reference to Osric's hat, now back on his head, and
also to Osric as a young upstart. (Young lapwings left their nests so
early they presumably still had their shells on their heads.)
191. comply with: show courtesy toward.
193. drossy: worthless.
194–98. got ... trial: knows the current slang and frivolous manners to win
popular approval, but these evaporate in times of trial.
205–06. If ... ready: If he is ready, then I am.
209. In happy time: at an opportune moment.
210–11. use ... entertainment: show courtesy.

Hamlet. I do not think so. Since he went into France
    I have been in continual practice; I shall win at   215
    the odds. But thou wouldst not think how ill all's
    here about my heart. But it is no matter.
Horatio. Nay, good my lord—
Hamlet. It is but foolery; but it is such a kind of
    gaingiving° as would perhaps trouble a woman.   220
Horatio. If your mind dislike anything, obey it. I
    will forestall their repair° hither and say you
    are not fit.
Hamlet. Not a whit, we defy augury. There's a
    special providence in the fall of a sparrow.° If it   225
    be now, 'tis not to come; if it be not to come, it will
    be now; if it be not now, yet it will come: the
    readiness is all. Since no man has aught of what
    he leaves, what is't to leave betimes?° Let be.°

Enter KING CLAUDIUS, QUEEN GERTRUDE, LAERTES, LORDS, OSRIC,
and ATTENDANTS *with foils and gauntlets.*

King.
    Come, Hamlet, come, and take this hand from me.   230

KING CLAUDIUS *puts* LAERTES' *hand into* HAMLET'S.

Hamlet.
    Give me your pardon, sir. I've done you wrong;
    But pardon't, as you are a gentleman.
    This presence° knows,
    And you must needs have heard, how I am punished
    With sore distraction. What I have done   235
    That might your nature,° honor, and exception°

---

220. **gaingiving:** misgiving.
222. **repair:** coming.
225. **providence ... sparrow:** See Matthew 10:29.
228–29. **has ... betimes:** knows anything of what he leaves behind, what
    does an early death matter?
229. **Let be:** Enough.
233. **presence:** royal assembly.

Roughly awake, I here proclaim was madness.
Was't Hamlet wronged Laertes? Never Hamlet.
If Hamlet from himself be ta'en away,
And when he's not himself does wrong Laertes,   240
Then Hamlet does it not, Hamlet denies it.
Who does it, then? His madness. If't be so,
Hamlet is of the faction that is wronged;
His madness is poor Hamlet's enemy.
Sir, in this audience,   245
Let my disclaiming from a purposed evil
Free me so far in your most generous thoughts
That I have shot my arrow o'er the house
And hurt my brother.
Laertes.   I am satisfied in nature,°
Whose motive in this case should stir me most   250
To my revenge. But in my terms of honor
I stand aloof, and will no reconcilement
Till by some elder masters of known honor
I have a voice and precedent° of peace
To keep my name ungored.° But till that time   255
I do receive your offered love like love,
And will not wrong it.
Hamlet.   I embrace it freely,
And will this brother's wager frankly play.
Give us the foils. Come on.
Laertes.   Come, one for me.
Hamlet.
I'll be your foil,° Laertes. In mine ignorance   260
Your skill shall, like a star i' the darkest night,

---

236. **nature:** personal feelings (see also line 249). **exception:** disapproval.
249. **in nature:** in regard to my feelings.
254. **voice and precedent:** authoritative decree.
255. **ungored:** unwounded.
260. **foil:** Hamlet is punning on another meaning of *foil,* "a contrasting background for a bright jewel."

Stick fiery off° indeed.

Laertes.   You mock me, sir.

Hamlet.

No, by this hand.

King.

Give them the foils, young Osric. Cousin Hamlet,
You know the wager?

Hamlet.   Very well, my lord.   265
Your Grace hath laid the odds o'° the weaker side.

King.

I do not fear it, I have seen you both;
But since he is bettered,° we have therefore odds.

Laertes.

This is too heavy; let me see another.

Hamlet.

This likes° me well. These foils have all a length?°   270

They prepare to play.

Osric.

Ay, my good lord.

King.

Set me the stoups of wine upon that table.
If Hamlet give the first or second hit,
Or quit in answer of the third exchange,°
Let all the battlements their ordnance fire;   275
The King shall drink to Hamlet's better breath,°
And in the cup an union° shall he throw
Richer than that which four successive kings
In Denmark's crown have worn. Give me the cups;
And let the kettle° to the trumpet speak,   280

---

262. **Stick fiery off:** stand out brightly.
266. **laid the odds o':** backed.
268. **bettered:** said to be better.
270. **likes:** pleases. **have ... length:** are all equal in length.
274. **quit ... exchange:** get even in the third bout.
276. **breath:** vigor.
277. **union:** large pearl.
280. **kettle:** kettledrum.

The trumpet to the cannoneer without,
The cannons to the heavens, the heaven to earth,
"Now the King drinks to Hamlet." Come, begin.
And you, the judges, bear a wary eye.

Hamlet.
Come on, sir.

Laertes.   Come, my lord.

They play.

Hamlet.   One.

Laertes.   No.

Hamlet.   Judgment!   285

Osric.
A hit, a very palpable hit.

Laertes.   Well, again!

King.
Stay, give me drink. Hamlet, this pearl is thine;
Here's to thy health.

Trumpets sound, and cannon shot off within.

                    Give him the cup.

Hamlet.
I'll play this bout first; set it by awhile.
Come.

They play.

              Another hit. What say you?   290

Laertes.
A touch, a touch; I do confess.

King.
Our son shall win.

Queen.   He's fat,° and scant of breath.
Here, Hamlet, take my napkin,° rub thy brows.
The Queen carouses to thy fortune, Hamlet.

Hamlet.
Good madam!

---

292.   **fat:** not in good condition.
293.   **napkin:** handkerchief.

King.   Gertrude, do not drink.   295
Queen.
  I will, my lord; I pray you pardon me.

She drinks.

King. [*Aside.*]
  It is the poisoned cup; it is too late.
Hamlet.
  I dare not drink yet, madam; by-and-by.
Queen.
  Come, let me wipe thy face.
Laertes.
  My lord, I'll hit him now.
King.   I do not think't.   300
Laertes. [*Aside.*]
  And yet 'tis almost against my conscience.
Hamlet.
  Come, for the third, Laertes! You but dally;
  I pray you pass° with your best violence;
  I am afeard you make a wanton of me.°
Laertes.
  Say you so? Come on.   305

They play.

Osric.
  Nothing neither way.
Laertes.
  Have at you now!

LAERTES *wounds* HAMLET; *then, in scuffling, they change rapiers,
and* HAMLET *wounds* LAERTES.

King.   Part them! They are incensed.
Hamlet.
  Nay, come! again!

QUEEN *falls.*

---

303. **pass:** thrust.
304. **make … me:** toy with me.

Osric.   Look to the Queen there, ho!
Horatio.
    They bleed on both sides. How is it, my lord?
Osric.
    How is't, Laertes?   310
Laertes.
    Why, as a woodcock to mine own springe,° Osric.
    I am justly killed with mine own treachery.
Hamlet.
    How does the Queen?
King.   She swoons to see them bleed.
Queen.
    No, no! the drink, the drink! O my dear Hamlet!
    The drink, the drink! I am poisoned.   315

She dies.

Hamlet.
    O villiany! Ho! let the door be locked.
    Treachery! Seek it out.

LAERTES *falls.*

Laertes.
    It is here, Hamlet. Hamlet, thou art slain;
    No med'cine in the world can do thee good.
    In thee there is not half an hour of life.   320
    The treacherous instrument is in thy hand,
    Unbated and envenomed. The foul practice°
    Hath turned itself on me. Lo, here I lie,
    Never to rise again. Thy mother's poisoned.
    I can no more. The King, the King's to blame.   325
Hamlet.
    The point envenomed too?
    Then, venom, to thy work.

Stabs KING.

---

311. **springe:** snare.
322. **practice:** ruse.

All. Treason! treason!
King.
O, yet defend me, friends! I am but hurt.
Hamlet.
Here, thou incestuous, murd'rous, damned Dane,   330
Drink off this potion. Is thy union here?
Follow my mother.

KING *dies.*

Laertes.   He is justly served.
It is a poison tempered by himself.
Exchange forgiveness with me, noble Hamlet.
Mine and my father's death come not upon thee,   335
Nor thine on me!

He dies.

Hamlet.
Heaven make thee free° of it! I follow thee.
I am dead, Horatio. Wretched Queen, adieu!
You that look pale and tremble at this chance,
That are but mutes° or audience to this act,   340
Had I but time (as this fell sergeant, Death,
Is strict in his arrest), O, I could tell you—
But let it be. Horatio, I am dead;
Thou liv'st; report me and my cause aright
To the unsatisfied.°
Horatio.   Never believe it.   345
I am more an antique Roman° than a Dane.
Here's yet some liquor left.
Hamlet.   As thou'rt a man,
Give me the cup. Let go! By heaven, I'll have't.
O good Horatio, what a wounded name,
Things standing thus unknown, shall live
        behind me!   350

337. **free:** absolved.
340. **mutes:** those with no parts to play.
345. **the unsatisfied:** those who don't yet know.
346. **antique Roman:** The ancient Romans preferred suicide to dishonor.

If thou didst ever hold me in thy heart,
Absent thee from felicity awhile,
And in this harsh world draw thy breath in pain,
To tell my story.

March afar off, and shot within.

What warlike noise is this?

Osric.
Young Fortinbras, with conquest come from Poland,   355
To the ambassadors of England gives
This warlike volley.

Hamlet.   O, I die, Horatio!
The potent poison quite o'ercrows° my spirit.
I cannot live to hear the news from England,
But I do prophesy the election lights   360
On Fortinbras. He has my dying voice.
So tell him, with th' occurrents,° more and less,
Which have solicited—° The rest is silence.

Hamlet dies.

Horatio.
Now cracks a noble heart. Good night sweet prince,
And flights of angels sing thee to thy rest!   365

March within.

Why does the drum come hither?

Enter FORTINBRAS, *the* ENGLISH AMBASSADORS, *and others.*

Fortinbras. Where is this sight?
Horatio.   What is it you would see?
If aught of woe or wonder,° cease your search.
Fortinbras.
This quarry cries on havoc.° O proud Death,

358: **o'ercrows:** triumphs over (crowing like a victorious rooster).
362. **occurents:** occurrences.
363. **solicited:** urged.
368. **wonder:** calamity.
369. **This … havoc:** This heap of bodies proclaims wanton slaughter.

What feast is toward in thine eternal cell   370
That thou so many princes at a shot
So bloodily hast struck?
First Ambassador.   The sight is dismal;°
And our affairs from England come too late.
The ears are senseless that should give us hearing
To tell him his commandment is fulfilled,   375
That Rosencrantz and Guildenstern are dead.
Where should we have our thanks?
Horatio.   Not from his mouth,
Had it the ability of life to thank you.
He never gave commandment for their death.
But since, so jump upon° this bloody question,°   380
You from the Polack wars, and you from England,
Are here arrived, give order that these bodies
High on a stage° be placed to the view;
And let me speak to the yet unknowing world
How these things came about. So shall you hear   385
Of carnal, bloody, and unnatural acts;
Of accidental judgments, casual° slaughters,
Of deaths put on° by cunning and forced cause;
And, in this upshot, purposes mistook
Fall'n on the inventors' heads. All this can I   390
Truly deliver.
Fortinbras.   Let us haste to hear it,
And call the noblest to the audience.
For me, with sorrow I embrace my fortune.
I have some rights of memory° in this kingdom,
Which now to claim my vantage doth invite me.°   .395
Horatio.
Of that I shall have also cause to speak,

---

372. **dismal:** dreadful.
380. **so jump upon:** at the exact moment of. **question:** affair.
383. **stage:** platform.
387. **casual:** chance.
388. **put on:** instigated.
394. **of memory:** unforgotten.
395. **now ... me:** favorable opportunity now invites me to claim.

And from his mouth whose voice will draw on more. °
But let this same be presently performed,
Even while men's minds are wild,° lest more mischance
On° plots and errors happen.

Fortinbras.   Let four captains   400
Bear Hamlet like a soldier to the stage;
For he was likely, had he been put on,°
To have proved most royally; and for his passage°
The soldiers' music and the rites of war
Speak loudly for him.   405
Take up the bodies. Such a sight as this
Becomes the field, but here shows much amiss.
Go, bid the soldiers shoot.

Exeunt, marching; after which a peal of ordnance is shot off.

---

397. **draw on more:** induce further voices (for Fortinbras).
399. **wild:** in turmoil.
400. **On:** as a result of.
402. **put on:** put to the test.
403. **for his passage:** to mark his passing.

CONNECTIONS

Just Lather, That's All

Hernando Téllez

He said nothing when he entered. I was passing the best of my razors back and forth on a strop. When I recognized him I started to tremble. But he didn't notice. Hoping to conceal my emotion, I continued sharpening the razor. I tested it on the meat of my thumb, and then held it up to the light. At that moment he took off the bullet-studded belt that his gun holster dangled from. He hung it up on a wall hook and placed his military cap over it. Then he turned to me, loosening the knot of his tie, and said, "It's hot as hell. Give me a shave." He sat in the chair.

I estimated he had a four-day beard. The four days taken up by the latest expedition in search of our troops. His face seemed reddened, burned by the sun. Carefully, I began to prepare the soap. I cut off a few slices, dropped them into the cup, mixed in a bit of warm water, and began to stir with the brush. Immediately the foam began to rise. "The other boys in the group should have this much beard, too." I continued stirring the lather.

"But we did all right, you know. We got the main ones. We brought back some dead, and we've got some others still alive. But pretty soon they'll all be dead."

"How many did you catch?" I asked.

"Fourteen. We had to go pretty deep into the woods to find them. But we'll get even. Not one of them comes out of this alive, not one." He leaned back on the chair when he saw me with the lather-covered brush in my hand. I still had to put the sheet on him. No doubt about it, I was upset. I took a sheet out of a drawer and knotted it around my customer's neck. He wouldn't stop talking. He probably thought I was in sympathy with his party.

"The town must have learned a lesson from what we did the other day," he said.

"Yes," I replied, securing the knot at his dark, sweaty neck.

"That was a fine show, eh?"

"Very good," I answered, turning back for the brush. The man closed his eyes with a gesture of fatigue and sat waiting for the cool caress of the soap. I had never had him so close to me. The day he ordered the whole town to file into the patio of the school to see the four rebels hanging there, I came face-to-face with him for an instant. But the sight of the mutilated bodies kept me from noticing the face of the man who had directed it all, the face I was now about to take into my hands. It was not an unpleasant face, certainly. And the beard, which made him seem a bit older than he was, didn't suit him badly at all. His name was Torres. Captain Torres. A man of imagination, because who else would have thought of hanging the naked rebels and then holding target practice on certain parts of their bodies? I began to apply the first layer of soap. With his eyes closed, he continued. "Without any effort I could go straight to sleep," he said, "but there's plenty to do this afternoon." I stopped the lathering and asked with a feigned lack of interest: "A firing squad?" "Something like that, but a little slower." I got on with the job of lathering his beard. My hands started trembling again. The man could not possibly realize it, and this was in my favor. But I would have preferred that he hadn't come. It was likely that many of our faction had seen him enter. And an enemy under one's roof imposes certain conditions. I would be obliged to shave that beard like any other one, carefully, gently, like that of any customer, taking pains to see that no single pore emitted a drop of blood. Being careful to see that the little tufts of hair did not lead the blade astray. Seeing that his skin

ended up clean, soft, and healthy, so that passing the back
of my hand over it I couldn't feel a hair. Yes, I was secretly a
rebel, but I was also a conscientious barber, and proud of
the preciseness of my profession. And this four days' growth
of beard was a fitting challenge.

I took the razor, opened up the two protective arms,
exposed the blade and began the job, from one of the side-
burns downward. The razor responded beautifully. His beard
was inflexible and hard, not too long, but thick. Bit by bit the
skin emerged. The razor rasped along, making its customary
sound as fluffs of lather mixed with bits of hair gathered
along the blade. I paused a moment to clean it, then took
up the strop again to sharpen the razor, because I'm a barber who does things properly. The man, who had kept his
eyes closed, opened them now, removed one of his hands
from under the sheet, felt the spot on his face where the
soap had been cleared off, and said, "Come to the school
today at six o'clock." "The same thing as the other day?" I
asked, horrified. "It could be better," he replied. "What do
you plan to do?" "I don't know yet. But we'll amuse ourselves." Once more he leaned back and closed his eyes. I
approached him with the razor poised. "Do you plan to
punish them all?" I ventured timidly. "All." The soap was
drying on his face. I had to hurry. In the mirror I looked
toward the street. It was the same as ever: the grocery store
with two or three customers in it. Then I glanced at the
clock: two twenty in the afternoon. The razor continued on
its downward stroke. Now from the other sideburn down.
A thick, blue beard. He should have let it grow like some
poets or priests do. It would suit him well. A lot of people
wouldn't recognize him. Much to his benefit, I thought,
as I attempted to cover the neck area smoothly. There, for
sure, the razor had to be handled masterfully, since the hair,
although softer, grew into little swirls. A curly beard. One of

the tiny pores could be opened up and issue forth its pearl of blood. A good barber such as I prides himself on never allowing this to happen to a client. And this was a first-class client. How many of us had he ordered shot? How many of us had he ordered mutilated? It was better not to think about it. Torres did not know that I was his enemy. He did not know it nor did the rest. It was a secret shared by very few, precisely so that I could inform the revolutionaries of what Torres was doing in the town and of what he was planning each time he undertook a rebel-hunting excursion. So it was going to be very difficult to explain that I had him right in my hands and let him go peacefully—alive and shaved.

The beard was now almost completely gone. He seemed younger, less burdened by years than when he had arrived. I suppose this always happens with men who visit barbershops. Under the stroke of my razor Torres was being rejuvenated—rejuvenated because I am a good barber, the best in the town, if I may say so. A little more lather here, under his chin, on his Adam's apple, on this big vein. How hot it is getting! Torres must be sweating as much as I. But he is not afraid. He is a calm man, who is not even thinking about what he is going to do with the prisoners this afternoon. On the other hand I, with this razor in my hands, stroking and restroking this skin, trying to keep blood from oozing from these pores, can't even think clearly. Damn him for coming, because I'm a revolutionary and not a murderer. And how easy it would be to kill him. And he deserves it. Does he? No! What the devil! No one deserves to have someone else make the sacrifice of becoming a murderer. What do you gain by it? Nothing. Others come along and still others, and the first ones kill the second ones and they the next ones and it goes on like this until everything is a sea of blood. I could cut this throat just so, zip!

zip! I wouldn't give him time to complain and since he has his eyes closed he wouldn't see the glistening knife blade or my glistening eyes. But I'm trembling like a real murderer. Out of his neck a gush of blood would spout onto the sheet, on the chair, on my hands, on the floor. I would have to close the door. And the blood would keep inching along the floor, warm, ineradicable, uncontainable, until it reached the street, like a little scarlet stream. I'm sure that one solid stroke, one deep incision, would prevent any pain. He wouldn't suffer. But what would I do with the body? Where would I hide it? I would have to flee, leaving all I have behind, and take refuge far away, far, far away. But they would follow until they found me. "Captain Torres' murderer. He slit his throat while he was shaving him—a coward." And then on the other side. "The avenger of us all. A name to remember. (And here they would mention my name.) He was the town barber. No one knew he was defending our cause."

And what of all this? Murderer or hero? My destiny depends on the edge of this blade. I can turn my hand a bit more, press a little harder on the razor, and sink it in. The skin would give way like silk, like rubber, like the strop. There is nothing more tender than human skin and the blood is always there, ready to pour forth. A blade like this doesn't fail. It is my best. But I don't want to be a murderer, no sir. You came to me for a shave. And I perform my work honorably. . . . I don't want blood on my hands. Just lather, that's all. You are an executioner and I am only a barber. Each person has his own place in the scheme of things. That's right. His own place.

Now his chin had been stroked clean and smooth. The man sat up and looked into the mirror. He rubbed his hands over his skin and felt it fresh, like new.

"Thanks," he said. He went to the hanger for his belt, pistol and cap. I must have been very pale; my shirt felt soaked. Torres finished adjusting the buckle, straightened his pistol in the holster and after automatically smoothing down his hair, he put on the cap. From his pants pocket he took out several coins to pay me for my services. And he began to head toward the door. In the doorway he paused for a moment, and turning to me he said:

"They told me that you'd kill me. I came to find out. But killing isn't easy. You can take my word for it." And he headed on down the street.

translated by Donald A. Yates

■ ■ ■

Plays and Performances
John Russell Brown

Before a new play was ready for performance much had
to be done. First, of course, was the writing, and for
Shakespeare we know this meant literary research as well
as the pleasures and pains of composition. He consulted
many books, some of them very large. If all the books
he used for *King Lear,* or one of the history plays, were
placed in a pile no one person could carry them without
some difficulty.

Once a script was finished, the author's 'fair copy'
would be made and sent first to the Actors' Company for
their approval. Then it had to go to the censor. No 'matters of state or religion' could be shown on the stage on
pain of imprisonment for the author and loss of licence
to perform for the actors. The Master of the Queen's (or
King's) Revels had to read and approve every word, at
the players' expense, before official approval was issued
for a new play. Yet even this did not prevent some theatres being closed for performing 'seditious, blasphemous
or scandalous' plays, and some dramatists, Ben Jonson
among them, suffered periods of imprisonment in consequence. At a time of unrest, when the Earl of Essex was
challenging the Queen's authority and armed bands ter-
rorized the streets of London, the Chamberlain's Men were
forbidden to perform *Richard the Second,* a play already
licensed and performed, because it contains a scene in
which a king is compelled to renounce his crown: in
1601, the Queen's counsellors believed that this might
encourage her enemies and spark off a revolution. The
theatre was taken very seriously by the authorities and
was allowed to deal with political issues only if they did

not refer too obviously to current affairs or seditious ideas, but were set, safely, in an earlier century or, better still, in ancient Rome or foreign countries.

A large proportion of the people of London provided the audience at the Globe. By the end of the sixteenth century, the city had some 160,000 inhabitants, and the combined capacity of the two theatres then in regular use was not less than 5,000 on each of the six days of a working week. This means that, discounting buildings used only occasionally for plays, if the average playgoer went once a fortnight and the two main theatres were a little more than half full, then one in every four or five Londoners patronized the theatre. When the two playhouses were full, in the middle of a normal week-day, one out of every thirty-two people would be found watching a performance while most of the remainder would be working.

The theatres had their fans who were so keen to see the first performance of a new play that the actors were able to charge double for admission on those occasions. And they had to change the repertoire very frequently to maintain this avid interest. Nearly all sorts of people came. An eye-witness has identified 'tailers, tinkers, cordwainers, sailors, old men, young men, women, boys, girls and such like' in the audience. When an investigation was made by the authorities, they found 'not only gentlemen and servingmen' among the audience, but also 'lawyers, clerks, country men that had law-cases, ay the Queen's men, knights and, as it was credibly reported, an Earl'.

The Mayor and Aldermen of the City of London tried to limit the number of performances in any one week, so that there was less absenteeism from work. Clergymen who believed that idle and expensive recreation was a sin, denounced the theatre as 'Satan's Synagogue' and the

'Nest of the Devil'. They also did what they could to pro-
hibit performances and exhort the people to attend to
their work—and to listen to sermons instead of plays.
Theatre-owners retaliated by choosing sites in the sub-
urbs, outside the City's jurisdiction, and the crowds followed them gladly.

Plays were printed, as well as staged, after further
scrutiny by official censors. Paperback books, measuring
about five by seven-and-a-half inches (or twelve and a
half by nineteen centimetres), were sold for sixpennies
each. Some authors actively encouraged this double sale
of their writings but, in order to prevent rival companies
from staging their successes, the actors tried to stop or at
least delay publication. Sales could be brisk: Shakespeare's
Richard the Second and *Richard the Third* each went
through five editions between 1597 and 1623. Although
many of his plays were first printed after his death, in the
complete edition of 1623, and although he took no personal interest in publication, sales of individual plays were
so good that Shakespeare was often the best-selling author,
topped only by sales of the Bible, prayer books and some
official publications.

When a new play had been licensed, the next task
was to distribute its parts. Shakespeare, as a sharer in the
actors' company, knew very well for whom he was writing, and some of the roles in his plays would cast themselves. Normally Richard Burbage would take the lead;
and the survival of their names in printed texts shows that
some of Shakespeare's manuscripts indicated that Kempe
the clown and Cowley, his 'feed', should perform certain
parts. Others were written especially for John Sinklo, an
exceptionally thin actor in the company.

Other jobs to be done for a new play included the
assembly of properties, the swords, purses, lanterns,

luggage, carts, tables, chairs, and other physical require-
ments of the text. Costumes had to be sorted out of stock,
or especially made, purchased or adapted, as appropriate.
Music for songs might have to be composed and arrange-
ments made for having a fire on stage or a procession
with many torches. A date had to be fixed for the first
performance. The 'book' had to be marked up with warn-
ings for the actors and properties to be ready and cues
for music and sound effects. This copy of the play
belonged to the 'book-keeper', who acted as prompter
and controlled backstage activity.

The actors were not given copies of the play, but
only of the words of their own parts with the briefest of
cues from preceding speeches. These 'parts' were taken
home to be studied and learned. Joint rehearsals were few,
except for the boy-actors with their respective masters. Each
character was separately prepared because the mornings
allotted to the rehearsals of each play had to be used for
arranging movement on and around the stage and for
sorting out costume-changes and the provision of properties, as well as tackling the physical problems of fighting,
banqueting, dancing, processing and other group activities
that were commonly required by the texts. There is some
evidence that authors 'instructed' the leading actors indi-
vidually, but for the most part a play was realised fully
only in performance before an audience: then the various
characters truly met and, with the encouragement of their
audience, the actors discovered what dramatic life and
excitement was possible. 'Scenical representation,' wrote
George Chapman, a dramatist a few years older than
Shakespeare, gives to any history a 'personal and exact
life' that adds 'lustre, spirit and apprehension'.

In a way unknown today, the actors and audience
held the play's fortunes in their hands. There was no

director to take charge and accept responsibility. So far
as we can tell from the day-to-day records of the rival
Admiral's Men, there was no 'run' or special 'production'
of a play at the Globe—neither word was known at the
time—but each afternoon a different play would be performed. During the 1594–5 season, the Admiral's Men
staged thirty-eight different plays, of which twenty-one
were new to the repertoire. In 1596–7, there were thirty-
four plays, fourteen of them new. Very occasionally a
great success was played twice in one week, but once or
twice a month was the usual frequency. Records of the
Chamberlain's and King's Men are not so complete, but
what has survived suggests a similar way of running the
repertory.

'Lustre, spirit and apprehension' would obviously
be required to perform this ever-changing programme:
the number of words the chief actors had to remember
is only the most obvious problem arising from such a
demanding schedule. Standard ways of staging various
types of scenes must have been developed, to be modified according to the demands of each text and the excitements of any one performance. But how nobly or
hurriedly, slowly, loudly, uncertainly or sensitively a hero
might die, would always be uncertain. When a play returned to the repertoire after a fortnight's break, the bal-
ance of the performances, the relative strength of this
character or that, could change almost out of recognition,
and in the new enactment the words of the dialogue
would surely be re-interpreted. The audience went to see
how the play was played, as well as what was played—
as at football a spectator is interested as much in the
quality of the game as in the result.

A trumpeter announced when everything was ready
for a performance by three calls from a special position

high above the tiring house. People still outside hurried in
to find last-minute places and, for a moment, the audito-
rium was hushed.

■ ■ ■

In a Dark Time
Theodore Roethke

In a dark time, the eye begins to see.
I meet my shadow in the deepening shade;
I hear my echo in the echoing wood—
A lord of nature weeping to a tree.
I live between the heron and the wren,
Beasts of the hill and serpents of the den.

What's madness but nobility of soul
At odds with circumstance? The day's on fire!
I know the purity of pure despair,
My shadow pinned against a sweating wall.
That place among the rocks—is it a cave,
Or winding path? The edge is what I have.

A steady storm of correspondences!
A night flowing with birds, a ragged moon,
And in broad day the midnight comes again!
A man goes far to find out what he is—
Death of the self in a long, tearless night,
All natural shapes blazing unnatural light.

Dark, dark my light, and darker my desire.
My soul, like some heat-maddened summer fly,
Keeps buzzing at the sill. Which I is *I*?
A fallen man, I climb out of my fear.
The mind enters itself, and God the mind,
And one is One, free in the tearing wind.

■ ■ ■

Raymond Chandler's Hamlet

Jonathan Vos Post

*Winner of Honorable Mention in the 1995
International Imitation Raymond Chandler Competition*

Something was rotten in Denmark, rank and gross, as rotten as a dame named Gertrude fooling around with her husband's killer while the caterer recycled the funeral baked meats for the wedding reception, at which the bride did not wear white.

Hamlet was sharp for a prince, good with a knife, but not sharp enough to handle his old man kicking the bucket with an earful of murder.

My name's Horatio, Hamlet's gumshoe buddy, trying to stay clean in a dirty castle. A grizzled ghost pleaded the Fifth when I gave him the third degree, then split the scene when the cock crew, like a guilty man before a marshall serving a summons.

King Claudius, cool as a cucumber after offing his brother, twisted nephew Hamlet's arm not to return to college at Wittenberg, Caltech not having yet been built.

The air bit shrewdly, it was very cold, when the ghost came again. It was Hamlet's father's spirit. His tale would freeze blood, pop out eyes, and make your hair stand on end like porcupine quills. He demanded revenge for murder most foul. The snake that killed him wore the crown. Me and Hamlet took the case.

Hamlet's main squeeze, Ophelia, a green girl, griped that Hamlet was pale as his shirt, in dirty sox, acting weird. . . . The sun bred maggots in a dead dog.

Hamlet played mad, but when the Santa Ana blew, he knew a hawk from a handsaw. A bunch of non-Guild actors showed up for the castle venue.

"To be or not to be," mused Hamlet, thinking of a one-way ticket to the morgue.

At the play, "The Murder of Gonzago," an actor dumped poison in the play-King's ear. The real King freaked. Polonius hid behind Queen Gertrude's bedroom curtain, but Hamlet smelled a rat and stabbed him dead.

"I'll lug the guts into the neighbor room," he said, then hid the corpse where worms ate brunch and didn't leave a tip.

I heard Ophelia do the hey-nonny-nonny gig, singing about flowers and Valentines, but a Valentine's Day Massacre was more like it. Laertes found his sister Ophelia, poor wretch, in the weeping brook, drowned in muddy death. It was time for the great axe to fall.

A couple of clowns found a skull a scream, when they tipped Ophelia into the grave. Hamlet jumped in on top of her. Hamlet and Laertes got down to business with a couple of long knives while the Queen gulped down some poison Pinot Noir the King meant for Hamlet.

The Queen falls. Hamlet and Laertes cut each other up, then Hamlet swigs from the deadly cup and stabs the King stone cold dead. Instant karma, I guess.

Rosencrantz and Guildenstern were snuffed. Fortinbras stomped into Denmark with his gang, and lots of drums.

I was the last guy left. I heard a gunshot. I looked off into the distance, a solid heavy man like a rock.

Then I began to wonder where my next paycheck was coming from.

■ ■ ■

from John Gielgud Directs Richard Burton in *Hamlet*

A Journal of Rehearsals

Richard L. Sterne

Thursday, January 30, 1964
3:30 P.M. Read-through of Act I

At 3:30 P.M. the company returned to the rehearsal hall. The O'Keefe rehearsal room is large; it fully duplicates the dimensions of its vast stage. Along one wall of the room was a row of full-length mirrors, used for dance rehearsals and now curtained. Two long folding tables had been set up at one end of the room. Behind the tables and filling up most of the 35-by-60-foot room were the actual platforms and stairways of the set, which in less than four weeks would be painted and moved upstairs to the stage for the opening night.

The company was seated around the tables. Twenty-four members were present—all but George Rose, George Voskovec, and Dillon Evans, who were called for later rehearsals. After a greeting by Mr. Cohen, Sir John began his introductory remarks:

GIELGUD   This afternoon I want to read through the first act, but I thought I'd begin by telling you a little of what I had in mind. When Richard asked me to do the play for him, I already had the idea that a Shakespeare play might be done as a run-through. So often it has been my experience in many plays that we have been through the whole play for the last time (in rehearsal) without interruptions; then, all of a sudden, the scenery and the lighting come, and everybody is thrown to pieces. And even after we have seen the sets, however beautiful they are, they sort of cramp the imagination and the poetry—and they are also apt to destroy the pace. So we are going to act the play as if it were the final run-through before the technical rehearsals begin, and play it in rehearsal clothes, stripped of all extraneous trappings.

I looked at this play very carefully and it seemed to me that by avoiding changes of scenery and by improvising all the accessories, we might force the audience to imagine a great deal that would be limited otherwise by specific scenery and properties.

Of course, we can't really have no lighting and no scenery. Ben Edwards has designed a set which looks like the walls of an empty theatre, with high, double-dock doors in the center at the back, and ropes and weights hanging from the grid. Some plain, rough rostrums will be arranged in front of the back wall, giving various levels and steps and ramps leading to exits left and right. The lighting must seem to be ordinary rehearsal lighting. But actually, as the play begins at night in the first scene, then goes to day for the court scene, then to evening for Ophelia, then back to the next night for the platform scene, then back to day again—so we propose to have the lights fade from day to night and rise from night to day, probably taking a quarter of an hour. But from the audience's point of view, there'll be no sudden blackouts, no sudden changes of light to startle them and disturb their concentration. I once saw a Shakespearean production done all through under white light, but I thought this became tedious after a few scenes.

Often, in rehearsal, one sees an actor pick up a
piece of material for a cloak, as it were, and fling it
over his shoulder convincingly, and he seems to
believe it more than when he has the final costume.
Actors seize on things that they need. If they suddenly
think they must have a cloak or a dagger or a sword,
they snatch a substitute from somewhere or even pretend to do so.

We will have a few beautiful period props—an
inkstand on the table, a portfolio for the King, and a
showy hat for Osric—these things we can use, and
since the people onstage will be dressed in ordinary
clothes, perhaps these things will suddenly seem more
interesting. And we shall take care with the colors used
for the clothing of the principals so that they will stand
out in exactly the same way that the royal family in
England stand out when they appear in public.

But I would like you to imagine that if there had
been costumes for this performance they would have
been Renaissance clothes of the time of Holbein—but
you see, you won't have the ruffs or the tights or the
wigs or the beards. I think it might be good if some
of the men grow their hair long, as if they were getting ready to wear a costume—it would be effective,
and most actors like their hair long. Too, if people
want to have beards, we may decide that beards are
good. Alfred [Drake] has a splendid beard already.
George Rose might have a beard. I don't think Polonius
[Hume Cronyn] needs a beard because when Hamlet
says "It shall to the barber's with your beard!" he can
simply flick his fingers rather than pull Polonius'
beard.

But I want the actors to help by using their imaginations. Everybody must try to find what he would

feel. I want the acting to be strong and broad and spoken out with all the poetry of the play. It should be realistic but strongly projected.

We have had brilliant productions of many of the classics in modern dress, but I have always felt that when the actors begin to have revolvers, cigarette holders, umbrellas, and all sorts of things which the audience associates with other periods, these are distractions. Yet if we have a sword strapped round us as we do at rehearsal while we are wearing trousers instead of tights, after a few minutes nobody will notice the trousers.

Now let's have a look at the model of the set. The rear doors are used only when we have entrances from the outside—when the Players come, when the Ghost appears, or in the Fortinbras scene. There will be different directions for the movement of the actors in the platform scenes from those in the court scenes, in order to give an illusion of different locale when the scene changes. For example, the first platform scene moves diagonally across the stage, and the first court scene moves straight up and down, or horizontally. For the costuming, I am going to have Jane [Greenwood], the costumer, watch very closely at rehearsals to see if we should wear duffle coats and fur hats and boots and things, and if we see people wearing something effective, we'll try to copy them, or have people use their own clothes. I'm always fascinated by the way actors try to get into a part. Don't feel that you must dress in rehearsal clothes that make you *look* the part, but dress in the clothes that help to make you *feel* the part.

Well, now let's start reading and see how far we get this afternoon. If anybody feels strongly about cuts, or if there are things that I've cut out that they would love to have back, I will do my best to put them back. The play should begin like a pistol shot. We don't want the usual striking bells and wind to give atmosphere. Francisco believes he has seen the Ghost and shouts out "Who's there?" suddenly and with great force. All right, let's begin. . . .

* * *

There was great excitement for the performance. Critics had come from Canada, the United States, and England. Many celebrities were present. With the exception of a few uneasy moments in the final duel, the show ran smoothly and was much applauded at the final curtain.

Mr. Cohen gave a party for the company following the performance in the lobby of the theatre. Several members of the cast stayed up to read the local reviews. There was little agreement in them, as the following excerpts illustrate:

BURTON—THE COMPLETE HAMLET

Rockets return from outer space burning white-hot. Richard Burton, orbiting out among the celluloid stars for almost ten years, plunged back on to the stage last night burning just as brightly. It was a magnificent re-entry to the theatre for the wayward Welshman in Sir John Gielgud's streamlined *Hamlet*. . . .

Burton's performance is a masterpiece. He is the closest we shall come in this generation to the complete Hamlet. . . . Above all he is triumphantly articulate. Burton's voice is a supremely tuned instrument that can thunder like drums and ring like swords. . . .

Sir John has dared parade upon the O'Keefe Centre a naked *Hamlet* bared down to the taut skin of the text.

And how that skin shines, once it's out from under its usual muffling trappings. On a scant but solid, partially un-painted scaffold of platform and stairs, the players pass in rough rehearsal clothes. . . . There is no pageantry about this production. . . . Groupings are blunt and basic, external movements pared to a minimum to reveal the swift thrust and eddy of action and idea within. It is as if the soul body of the play was sliced open to disclose the heart clenching spasmodically, nerves twitching and writhing. . . .

Things lag only when Burton is out of sight. And that is because he is surrounded by such a startlingly weak company. Hume Cronyn is an exception. His Polonius is superbly shaped. . . .

Sir John intervenes in his own production only once as the ghost of the elder Hamlet and only here does a disturbing note of gimmickry intrude. . . . The only indication of his spectre's arrival is the opening and closing of the huge doors at the rear, which seems a rather clumsy way for a spirit to get about.

Ron Evans,
The Toronto Telegram

BURTON DISAPPOINTING

There is no doubt at any time that Richard Burton is an actor big enough to undertake the role, a fact not always true of modern Hamlets. He has great personal magnetism, a superb voice and a fund of wit as well as intelligence. Given all these attributes one is still aware that last night's was a disappointing performance.

Burton's Hamlet has gusts of greatness, flashes of intensity, touches of humanity and occasional depths of thought. But there were other passages that seemed loosely related to a central concept. . . .

The great soliloquies are spoken with imagination and intelligence, never as set pieces marking the progress of an actor, yet they do not strike deep into our hearts.

. . . The quality of speech that made Gielgud a great Hamlet served this production notably as the late King Hamlet. The device of a disembodied voice is impressive, but a speechless invisible Ghost proved hard to accept at first.

The absent Gielgud was one of three memorable performances. The other two were from Hume Cronyn as Polonius and George Rose as the Gravedigger. . . . The other major roles perhaps suffered in relationship with Burton's Hamlet. . . .

Ben Edwards' backstage setting supplies much of the evening's beauty, coupled with the sparse, always expressive groupings of the Gielgud direction. The bare platforms are immensely useful in shape, and the high brick backing—centered on two towering scene-doors—achieves lofty beauty in Jean Rosenthal's fitful lighting. Jane Greenwood's choice of modern rehearsal wear is tasteful and subtle. In fact, one is put off rather by the touches of costume than by the absence of it in a production which principally demonstrates that a well-understood play needs no frills, but that a great Hamlet demands great playing from even the best of actors.

Herbert Whittaker,
The Globe and Mail

HAMLET UNDONE

Any discussion of Sir John Gielgud's production of *Hamlet* must start with the bold fact that as of its pre-Broadway opening last night at the O'Keefe Centre it is an unmitigated disaster. . . .

Certainly as Richard Burton is handling Hamlet at the moment . . . he has no substantial or living quality. There Mr. Burton is on the stage, a performer of the most unmistakable physical and vocal power, but his movements have an inner slackness and his hands carry on private conversations. . . . The voice is diminished in its effectiveness by a persistent rasp. His is a performance, right now, without a controlling point of view to the extent that he has any identity at all. . . .

Most of the other performers are manifestly his inferior. . . . George Rose displays a mild competence in the actor-proof part of the First Gravedigger, and Hume Cronyn is singular in the cast in evincing some idea of the point of his character. . . .

If there is one thing the show doesn't have it is any sense of actors working towards a common purpose. However close they are to one another on the center stage, each performer in *Hamlet* occupies a self-contained unrelated world.

The list of short-comings extends much further, however. The stage is formless—an assortment of turbulent and familiar effects floating about at random. The set is an eyesore. The costuming makes no sense. The performance throughout is a parade of artistic horrors. Its main redeeming feature, and that will not do, is that it is well meant.

Nathan Cohen,
The Toronto Star

■ ■ ■

Two Poems by Maya Angelou

Insomniac

There are some nights when
sleep plays coy,
aloof and disdainful.
And all the wiles
that I employ to win
its service to my side
are useless as wounded pride,
and much more painful.

Mourning Grace

If today I follow death,
go down its trackless wastes,
salt my tongue on hardened tears
for my precious dear time's waste
race
along that promised cave in a headlong
deadlong
haste,
Will you
have
the
grace
to mourn for
me?

■ ■ ■

The Olivier *Hamlet*

Bosley Crowther

September 1948

It may come as something of a rude shock to the theatre's traditionalists to discover that the tragedies of Shakespeare can be eloquently presented on the screen. So bound have these poetic dramas long been to the culture of our stage that the very thought of their transference may have staggered a few profound die-hards. But now the matter is settled; the filmed *Hamlet* of Laurence Olivier gives absolute proof that these classics are magnificently suited to the screen.

Indeed, this fine British-made picture, which opened at the Park Avenue last night under the Theatre Guild's elegant aegis, is probably as vivid and as clear an exposition of the doleful Dane's dilemma as modern-day playgoers have seen. And just as Olivier's ingenious and spectacular *Henry V* set out new visual limits for Shakespeare's historical plays, his *Hamlet* envisions new vistas in the great tragedies of the Bard.

It is not too brash or insensitive to say that these eloquent plays, in their uncounted stage presentations, have been more often heard than seen. The physical nature of the theatre, from the time of the Globe until now, has compelled that the audiences of Shakespeare listen more closely than they look. And, indeed, the physical distance of the audience from the stage has denied it the privilege of partaking in some of the most intimate moments of the plays.

But just as Olivier's great *Henry* took the play further away by taking it out into the open—and thereby revealed it visually—his *Hamlet* makes the play more evident by bringing it closer to you. The subtle reactions of the characters, the movements of their faces and forms, which can be so dramatically expressive and which are more or less remote on the stage, are here made emotionally incisive by their normal proximity. Coupled with beautiful acting and inspired interpretations all the way, this visual closeness to the drama offers insights that are brilliant and rare.

Further, a quietly-moving camera which wanders intently around the vast and gloomy palace of Elsinore, now on the misty battlements, now in the great council chamber, now in the bedroom of the Queen, always looking and listening, from this and from that vantage point, gives the exciting impression of a silent observer of great events, aware that big things are impending and anxious not to miss any of them.

Actually, a lot of material which is in the conventional *Hamlet* text is missing from the picture—a lot of lines and some minor characters, notably those two fickle windbags, Rosencrantz and Guildenstern. And it is natural that some fond Shakespearians are going to be distressed at the suddenly discovered omission of this or that memorable speech. But some highly judicious editing has not done damage to the fullness of the drama nor to any of its most familiar scenes. In fact, it has greatly speeded the unfolding of the plot and has given much greater clarity to its noted complexities.

Hamlet is nobody's glass-man, and the dark and troubled workings of his mind are difficult, even for Freudians. But the openness with which he is played by Mr. Olivier in this picture makes him reasonably comprehensible. His is no cold and sexless Hamlet. He is a solid and virile young man, plainly tormented by the anguish and the horror of a double shock. However, in this elucidation, it is more his wretched dismay at the treachery of his mother than at the death of his father that sparks his woe. And it is this disillusion in women that

shapes his uncertain attitude toward the young and mis-
guided Ophelia, a victim herself of a parent's deceit.

In the vibrant performance of Eileen Herlie as the Queen
is this concept evidenced, too, for plainly she shows the strain
and heartache of a ruptured attachment to her son. So
genuine is her disturbance that the uncommon evidence
she gives that she knows the final cup is poisoned before
she drinks it makes for heightened poignancy. And the
luminous performance of Jean Simmons as the truly fair
Ophelia brings honest tears for a shattered romance which
is usually a so-what affair.

No more than passing mention can be made at this
point of the fine work done by Norman Wooland as Horatio
and by Basil Sydney as the King, by Felix Aylmer as Polonius,
Terence Morgan as Laertes and all the rest. Perfect articula-
tion is only one thing for which they can be blessed. A
word, too, of commendation for the intriguing musical
score of William Walton and for the rich designing of Roger
Furse must suffice. In the straight black-and-white photog-
raphy which Mr. Olivier has wisely used—wisely, we say,
because the study is largely in somber mood—the palace
conceived for this *Hamlet* is a dark and haunted palace. It is
the grim and majestic setting for an uncommonly galvanic
film.

■ ■ ■

Fear No More the Heat o' the Sun

William Shakespeare

This song is from Shakespeare's play Cymbeline, *a romance set in ancient Britain. It is an elegy sung by Guiderius and Arviragus, the sons of the British king Cymbeline, for the royal page Fidele. (Fidele, who is mistakenly believed dead, is actually Imogen, the play's heroine, in disguise.) The critic Hallett Smith has described the song as "quite possibly the most resonant lyric lines Shakespeare ever composed."*

Guiderius

Fear no more the heat o' the sun,
　　Nor the furious winter's rages;
Thou thy worldly task hast done,
　　Home art gone, and ta'en thy wages:
Golden lads and girls all must,
As chimney-sweepers, come to dust.

Arviragus

Fear no more the frown o' the great;
　　Thou are past the tyrant's stroke;
Care no more to clothe and eat;
　　To thee the reed is as the oak:
The scepter, learning, physic, must
All follow this, and come to dust.

Guiderius

Fear no more the lightning-flash,

Arviragus

Nor the all-dreaded thunder-stone;

Guiderius

Fear not slander, censure rash;

Arviragus

Thou hast finished joy and moan:

Both

All lovers young, all lovers must
Consign to thee, and come to dust.

Guiderius

No exorciser harm thee!

Arviragus

Nor no witchcraft charm thee!

Guiderius

Ghost unlaid forbear thee!

Arviragus

Nothing ill come near thee!

Both

Quiet consummation have;
And renownèd be thy grave!

—from *Cymbeline,* Act IV, Scene 2,
lines 258–281

■ ■ ■

The Gibson *Hamlet*

Roger Ebert

January 1991

I had a professor in college who knew everything there was to know about *Romeo and Juliet.* Maybe he knew too much. One day in class he said he would give anything to be able to read it again for the first time. I feel the same way about *Hamlet.* I know the play so well by now, have seen it in so many different styles and periods and modes of dress, that it's like listening to a singer doing an old standard. You know the lyrics, so the only possible surprises come from style and phrasing.

The style of Franco Zeffirelli's *Hamlet,* with Mel Gibson in the title role, is robust and physical and—don't take this the wrong way—upbeat. Gibson doesn't give us another Hamlet as Mope, a melancholy Dane lurking in shadows and bewailing his fate. We get the notion, indeed, that there was nothing fundamentally awry with Hamlet until everything went wrong in his life, until his father died and his mother married his uncle with unseemly haste. This is a prince who was healthy and happy and could have lived a long and active life, if things had turned out differently.

Part of that approach may come from Zeffirelli, whose famous film version of *Romeo and Juliet* also played on the youth and attractiveness of its characters, who were bursting with life and romance until tragedy separated them. The approach also may come from Gibson himself, the most good-humored of contemporary stars, whose personal style is to deflect seriousness with a joke, and who doesn't easily descend into self-pity and morose masochism. He gives us a Hamlet who does his best to carry on, until he is overwhelmed by the sheer weight of events.

Zeffirelli sets his film in a spectacular location—a castle on an outcropping of the stark coast in northern Scotland, perched on top of a rock nearly surrounded by the sea. There is mud here, and rain and mist, and the characters sometimes seemed dragged down by the sheer weight of their clothing. This is a substantial world of real physical presence, fleshed out by an unusual number of extras; we have the feeling that this throne rules over real subjects, instead of existing only in Shakespeare's imagination.

Right at the outset, Zeffirelli and his collaborator on the shooting script, Christopher De Vore, take a liberty with *Hamlet* by shifting some dialogue and adding a few words to create a scene that does not exist in the original: The wake of Hamlet's father, with Hamlet, Gertrude and Claudius confronting each other over the coffin. In film terms, this scene makes the central problem of *Hamlet* perfectly clear, and dramatically strengthens everything that follows. It sets up not only Hamlet's anguish, but the real attraction between his mother and his uncle, which is seen in this version to be at least as sexual as it is political.

The cast is what is always called "distinguished," which usually but not always means "British," and includes at least three actors who have played Hamlet themselves: Alan Bates, as Claudius; Paul Scofield, as the ghost of Hamlet's father, and Ian Holm, as Polonius. Holm is especially effective in the "to thine own self be true" speech, evoking memories of his great work as the track coach in *Chariots of Fire,* and I enjoyed Bates' strength of bluster and lust, as a man of action who will have what he desires and not bother himself with the sorts of questions that torture Hamlet.

The women of the play, Glenn Close, as Gertrude, and Helena Bonham-Carter, as Ophelia, are both well cast. Close in particular adds an element of true mothering that is sometimes absent from Gertrude. She loves her son and cares for him, and is not simply an unfaithful wife with a short memory. Indeed, there are subtle physical suggestions that she has loved her son too closely, too warmly, creating the buried incestuous feelings that are the real spring of Hamlet's actions. Why has she remarried with such haste? Perhaps simply so the kingdom's power vacuum will be filled; she seems a sensible sort, and indeed everyone in this version seems fairly normal, if only Hamlet could rid himself of his gnawing resentment and shameful desires long enough to see it.

Bonham-Carter is a small and darkly beautiful actress who is effective at seeming to respond to visions within herself. As Ophelia she has a most difficult role to play, because a character who has gone mad can have no further relationship with the other characters but must essentially become a soloist. All of her later scenes are with herself.

That leaves Hamlet and his best friend, Horatio (Stephen Dillane), as those who are not satisfied with the state of things in the kingdom, and Dillane, with his unforced natural acting, provides a good partner for Gibson. As everything leads to the final sword fight and all of its results, as Hamlet's natural good cheer gradually weakens under the weight of his thoughts, the movie proceeds logically through its emotions. We never feel, as we do sometimes with other productions, that events happen arbitrarily. Zeffirelli's great contribution in "popularizing" the play has been to make it clear to the audience why events are unfolding as they are.

This *Hamlet* finally stands or falls on Mel Gibson's performance, and I think it will surprise some viewers with its strength and appeal. He has not been overawed by Shakespeare, has not fallen into a trap of taking this role too solemnly and lugubriously. He has observed the young man of the earlier and less troubled scenes, and started his performance from there, instead of letting every nuance be a foreshadow of what is to come. It's a strong, intelligent performance, filled with life, and it makes this into a surprisingly robust *Hamlet.*

■ ■ ■

The Branagh *Hamlet*

Roger Ebert

January 1997

There is early in Kenneth Branagh's *Hamlet* a wedding celebration, the Danish court rejoicing at the union of Claudius and Gertrude. The camera watches, and then pans to the right, to reveal the solitary figure of Hamlet, clad in black. It always creates a little shock in the movies when the foreground is unexpectedly occupied. We realize the subject of the scene is not the wedding, but Hamlet's experience of it. And we enjoy Branagh's visual showmanship: In all of his films, he reveals his joy in theatrical gestures.

His *Hamlet* is long but not slow, deep but not difficult, and it vibrates with the relief of actors who have great things to say, and the right ways to say them. And in the 70-mm. version, it has a visual clarity that is breathtaking. It is the first uncut film version of Shakespeare's most challenging tragedy, the first 70-mm. film since *Far and Away* in 1992, and at 238 minutes the second-longest major Hollywood production (one minute shorter than *Cleopatra*). Branagh's Hamlet lacks the narcissistic intensity of Laurence Olivier's (in the 1948 Academy Award winner), but the film as a whole is better, placing Hamlet in the larger context of royal politics, and making him less a subject for pity.

The story provides a melodramatic stage for inner agonies. Hamlet (Branagh), the prince of Denmark, mourns the untimely death of his father. His mother, Gertrude, rushes with unseemly speed into marriage with Claudius, her husband's brother. Something is rotten in the state of Denmark. And then the ghost of Hamlet's father appears and says he was poisoned by Claudius.

What must Hamlet do? He desires the death of Claudius but lacks the impulse to act out. He despises himself for his passivity. In tormenting himself he drives his mother to despair, kills Polonius by accident, speeds the kingdom toward chaos and his love, Ophelia, toward madness.

What is intriguing about *Hamlet* is the ambiguity of everyone's motives. Tom Stoppard's *Rosenkrantz and Guildenstern Are Dead* famously filtered all the action through the eyes of Hamlet's treacherous school friends. But how does it all look to Gertrude? To Claudius? To the heartbroken Ophelia? The great benefit of this full-length version is that these other characters become more understandable.

The role of Claudius (Derek Jacobi) is especially enriched: In shorter versions, he is the scowling usurper who functions only as villain. Here, with lines and scenes restored, he seems more balanced and powerful. He might have made a plausible king of Denmark, had things turned out differently. Yes, he killed his brother, but regicide was not unknown in medieval times, and perhaps the old king was ripe for replacement; this production shows Gertrude (Julie Christie) as lustfully in love with Claudius. By restoring the original scope of Claudius' role, Branagh emphasizes court and political intrigue instead of enclosing the material in a Freudian hothouse.

The movie's very sets emphasize the role of the throne as the center of the kingdom. Branagh uses costumes to suggest the 19th century, and shoots his exteriors at Blenheim Castle, seat of the duke of Marlborough and Winston Churchill's childhood home. The interior sets, designed by Tim Harvey and Desmond Crowe, feature a throne room surrounded by mirrored walls, overlooked by a gallery and divided by an elevated walkway. The set puts much of the action onstage (members of the court are constantly observing) and allows for intrigue (some of the mirrors are two-way, and lead to concealed chambers and corridors).

In this very public arena Hamlet agonizes, and is ob-served. Branagh uses rapid cuts to show others reacting to his words and meanings. And he finds new ways to stage familiar scenes, renewing the material. Hamlet's most famous soliloquy ("To be or not to be . . .") is delivered into a mir-ror, so that his own indecision is thrust back at him. When he torments Ophelia, a most private moment, we spy on them from the other side of a two-way mirror; he crushes her cheek against the glass and her frightened breath clouds it. When he comes upon Claudius at his prayers, and can kill him, many productions imagine Hamlet lurking behind a pillar in a chapel. Branagh is more intimate, showing a dagger blade insinuating itself through the mesh of a confessional.

One of the surprises of this uncut *Hamlet* is the crucial role of the play within the play. Many productions reduce the visiting troupe of actors to walk-ons; they provide a hook for Hamlet's advice to the players, and merely suggest the performance that Hamlet hopes will startle Claudius into betraying himself. Here, with Charlton Heston magnificently assured as the Player King, we listen to the actual lines of his play (which shorter versions often relegate to dumb-show at the back of the stage). We see how ingeniously and clev-erly they tweak the conscience of the king, and we see Claudius' pained reactions. The episode becomes a turning point; Claudius realizes that Hamlet is on to him.

As for Hamlet, Branagh (like Mel Gibson in the 1991 film) has no interest in playing him as an apologetic mope. Branagh is an actor of exuberant physical gifts and energy (when the time comes, his King Lear will bound about the heath). Consider the scene beginning "Oh, what a rogue and peasant knave am I . . . ," in which Hamlet bitterly regrets

■■

his inaction. The lines are delivered not in bewilderment but in mounting anger, and it is to Branagh's credit that he pulls out all the stops; a quieter Hamlet would make a tamer *Hamlet.*

Kate Winslet is touchingly vulnerable as Ophelia, red-nosed and snuffling, her world crumbling about her. Richard Briers makes Polonius not so much a foolish old man as an adviser out of his depth. Of the familiar faces, the surprise is Heston: How many great performances have we lost while he visited the Planet of the Apes? Billy Crystal is a surprise, but effective, as the grave digger. But Robin Williams, Jack Lemmon and Gerard Depardieu are distractions, their performances not overcoming our shocks of recognition.

At the end of this *Hamlet,* I felt at last as if I was getting a handle on the play (I never expect to fully understand it). It has been a long journey. I read it in high school, underlining the famous lines. I saw the Richard Burton film version, and later Olivier's. I studied it in graduate school. I have seen it onstage in England and the United States (most memorably in Aidan Quinn's punk version, when he scrawled graffiti on the wall: "2B = ?"). Franco Zeffirelli's version with Gibson came in 1991. I learned from them all.

One of the tasks of a lifetime is to become familiar with the great plays of Shakespeare. *Hamlet* is the most opaque. Branagh's version moved me, entertained me and made me feel for the first time at home in that doomed royal court. I may not be able to explain Hamlet, but at last I have a better idea than Rosencrantz and Guildenstern.

■ ■ ■

Sonnet 146

William Shakespeare

My soul, the center of my mortal life,

Poor soul, the center of my sinful earth,

rebels against the darkness of naught

My sinful earth, these rebel powers that thee array,

Why dost thou pine within and suffer dearth,

Painting thy outward walls so costly gay?

→ Why so large cost, having so short a lease,

Dost thou upon thy fading mansion spend? —

Shall worms, inheritors of this excess,

Eat up thy charge? Is this thy body's end?

Then, soul, live thou upon thy servant's loss,

And let that pine to aggravate thy store.

Buy terms divine in selling hours of dross,

a glittering pretence

Within be fed, without be rich no more.

knowledge

So shalt thou feed on Death, that feeds on men,

And Death once dead, there's no more dying then.

And need not the flagrant

■ ■ ■

Excesses of greed.

Wealth is found in knowledge

Riches are a mirage of greed.

poor man

William Shakespeare

(1564–1515)

He is the most famous writer in the world, but he left us
no journals or letters—only his poems and plays. What
we know about William Shakespeare's personal life comes
mostly from church and legal documents—a baptismal
registration, a marriage license, and records of real-estate
transactions. We also have a few remarks that others
wrote about him during his lifetime.

We know that William was born the third of eight
children, around April 23, 1564, in Stratford-on-Avon,
a market town about one hundred miles northwest of
London. His father, John, was a shopkeeper and a man of
some importance in Stratford, serving at various times as
justice of the peace and high bailiff (mayor).

William attended grammar school, where he studied
Latin grammar, Latin literature, and rhetoric (the uses of lan-
guage). As far as we know, he had no further formal edu-
cation. At the age of eighteen he married Anne Hathaway,
who was eight years older than he. Some time after the
birth of their second and third children (twins), Shakespeare
moved to London, apparently leaving his family in Stratford.

We know that several years later, by 1592, Shakespeare
had become an actor and a playwright. By 1594, he was
a charter member of a theatrical company called the Lord
Chamberlain's Men, which later became the King's Men.
Shakespeare worked with this company for the rest of
his writing life. Year after year he provided it with plays,
almost on demand. Shakespeare was the ultimate profes-
sional writer. He had a theater that needed plays, actors
who needed parts, and a family that needed to be fed.

Shakespeare probably wrote *Hamlet* in about 1600, roughly the midpoint of his formidable career. Earlier plays included *Richard III, Romeo and Juliet, A Midsummer Night's Dream,* and *Julius Caesar.* Later plays included *Othello, King Lear, Macbeth,* and *The Tempest. Hamlet* is often considered Shakespeare's greatest play, acclaimed for its psychological insight, wonderful poetry, and masterful construction.

Shakespeare died on April 23, 1616, possibly right on his fifty-second birthday. He is buried under the old stone floor in the chancel of Holy Trinity Church in Stratford. Carved on a stone over his grave is the following verse (spelling modified):

Good Friend, for Jesus' sake forbear
To dig the dust enclosed here.
Blessed be the man that spares these stones
And cursed be he that moves my bones.

These are hardly the best of Shakespeare's lines (if indeed they are his at all), but like his other lines, they seem to have worked: His bones lie undisturbed to this day. Yet Shakespeare lives on, for his plays are still frequently produced all over the world.

■ ■ ■